Stem Cell Research in Asia

The great hurry to realise promised cures in stem cell research requires regulation to guarantee bioethical research practices. Yet, increasingly similar national guidelines for stem cell research yields a range of diverging research practices. This book shows how the different rationale of regulation affects stem cell research practices in Asia. In low- and medium-income countries such as India and China the advancement of science has a different weight on the national agenda, and the evaluation of scientific research is measured with a different yardstick, depending on the political and national research environment. For developing countries the question of research funding into stem cell research, healthcare, and the donation of embryos, foetuses and oocytes entails different considerations compared to affluent welfare societies. Moreover, research institutions have different cultural and political histories, so that the meaning of formal guidelines, legislation and social rules may differ according to their various institutional settings. This volume discusses the informal cultures, social conventions and traditions that are crucial to the way in which stem cell research takes place in Asia.

This book was originally published as a special issue of *New Genetics and Society*.

Margaret Sleeboom-Faulkner is Professor of Social and Medical Anthropology at the University of Sussex, Brighton, UK. Her work focuses on processes of nation-state building in China and Japan and on biotechnology and society in Asia. She directs the Centre for Bionetworking and two projects on the life sciences in Asia. See: www.sussex.ac.uk/profiles/192052/research

Stem Cell Research in Asia
Looking Beyond Regulatory Exteriors

Edited by
Margaret Sleeboom-Faulkner

Routledge
Taylor & Francis Group

LONDON AND NEW YORK

First published 2015 by Routledge

2 Park Square, Milton Park, Abingdon, Oxfordshire OX14 4RN
711 Third Avenue, New York, NY 10017

Routledge is an imprint of the Taylor & Francis Group, an informa business

First issued in paperback 2018

British Library Cataloguing in Publication Data
A catalogue record for this book is available from the British Library

ISBN 13: 978-1-138-82931-2 (hbk)
ISBN 13: 978-1-138-37956-5 (pbk)

Typeset in Times New Roman
by RefineCatch Limited, Bungay, Suffolk

Publisher's Note
The publisher accepts responsibility for any inconsistencies that may have
arisen during the conversion of this book from journal articles to book chapters,
namely the possible inclusion of journal terminology.

Disclaimer
Every effort has been made to contact copyright holders for their permission to
reprint material in this book. The publishers would be grateful to hear from any
copyright holder who is not here acknowledged and will undertake to rectify
any errors or omissions in future editions of this book.

Contents

CONTENTS

Citation Information

The chapters in this book were originally published in *New Genetics and Society*, volume 30, issue 2 (June 2011); and issue 3 (September 2011). When citing this material, please use the original page numbering for each article, as follows:

Chapter 1
Editorial: Stem cell research in Asia: looking beyond regulatory exteriors
Margaret Sleeboom-Faulkner
New Genetics and Society, volume 30, issue 2 (June 2011) pp. 137–140

Chapter 2
The proliferation of stem cell therapies in post-Mao China: problematizing ethical regulation
Priscilla Song
New Genetics and Society, volume 30, issue 2 (June 2011) pp. 141–154

Chapter 3
Recruiter-patients as ambiguous symbols of health: bionetworking and stem cell therapy in India
Prasanna Kumar Patra and Margaret Sleeboom-Faulkner
New Genetics and Society, volume 30, issue 2 (June 2011) pp. 155–166

Chapter 4
Exploring appropriation of "surplus" ova and embryos in Indian IVF clinics
Jyotsna A. Gupta
New Genetics and Society, volume 30, issue 2 (June 2011) pp. 167–180

Chapter 5
Modalities of value, exchange, solidarity: the social life of stem cells in China
Achim Rosemann
New Genetics and Society, volume 30, issue 2 (June 2011) pp. 181–192

Chapter 6
Scientific institutions and effective governance: a case study of Chinese stem cell research
Joy Yueyue Zhang
New Genetics and Society, volume 30, issue 2 (June 2011) pp. 193–207

Chapter 7
"Your problem is that your face reveals everything when you are lying": making and remaking of conduct in South Korean life sciences
Leo Kim
New Genetics and Society, volume 30, issue 3 (September 2011) pp. 213–226

Chapter 8
Regulating cell lives in Japan: avoiding scandal and sticking to nature
Margaret Sleeboom-Faulkner
New Genetics and Society, volume 30, issue 3 (September 2011) pp. 227–240

Chapter 9
Reconsidering ethical issues about "voluntary egg donors" in Hwang's case in global context
Azumi Tsuge and Hyunsoo Hong
New Genetics and Society, volume 30, issue 3 (September 2011) pp. 241–252

Chapter 10
Biological scarcity: looking beyond regulatory exteriors in Taiwan
Jennifer A. Liu
New Genetics and Society, volume 30, issue 3 (September 2011) pp. 253–265

Chapter 11
Overcoming embryonic exceptionalism? Lessons from analyzing human stem cell research regulation in Israel
Barbara Prainsack
New Genetics and Society, volume 30, issue 3 (September 2011) pp. 266–277

Chapter 12
Looking beyond the regulatory exteriors of stem cell research in Asia – discussion
Margaret Sleeboom-Faulkner
New Genetics and Society, volume 30, issue 3 (September 2011) pp. 279–288

Please direct any queries you may have about the citations to
clsuk.permissions@cengage.com

Notes on Contributors

Jyotsna A. Gupta, University for Humanist Studies, Utrecht, The Netherlands.

Hyunsoo Hong, Department of Sociology, Meijigakuin University, Tokyo, Japan.

Leo Kim, School of Global Studies/SPRU, University of Sussex, UK.

Prasanna Kumar Patra, Department of Anthropology, Utkal University, Bhubaneswar, India.

Jennifer A. Liu, Department of Anthropology, University of Waterloo, Ontario, Canada.

Barbara Prainsack, School of Social Science & Public Policy, King's College London, London, UK.

Achim Rosemann, Department of Anthropology, University of Sussex, Brighton, UK.

Margaret Sleeboom-Faulkner, Department of Anthropology, University of Sussex, Brighton, UK.

Priscilla Song, Department of Anthropology, Washington University, St. Louis, USA.

Azumi Tsuge, Department of Sociology, Meijigakuin University, Tokyo, Japan.

Joy Yueyue Zhang, School of Social Policy, Sociology and Social Research (SSPSSR), University of Kent, UK.

INTRODUCTION

Stem cell research in Asia: looking beyond regulatory exteriors

This double special issue concerns the embedding of stem cell research in Asian societies: by examining the interplay between regulation and the contexts in which it is given meaning and affects the people that use the regulation, the special issue looks beyond formal regulatory guidelines for stem cell research. Much debate has been held on the regulatory, ethical and philosophical aspects of stem cell research, which usually emphasizes the political, moral and organizational aspects of the research. These discussions often study the decisions made by individual persons, ignoring the particular cultural and socio-political contexts of debates on regulation. In some cases, philosophical perspectives on bioethics project the ideologies of particular political cultures on to society. Thus, Confucian approaches advocate a Confucian society and utilitarian approaches advocate a society based on "free choice" (Sleeboom-Faulkner 2007, 2010). Rather than looking for ethical principles, this special issue tries to understand bioethical principles and research regulation in their societal embedding, which includes the socio-economic and politico-ideological aspects of the society. Contributors to the special issue, then, adopt an empirical approach to the study of stem cell research, using various methods based on fieldwork and interviews to fortify our insight into the practical workings of bioethics in societies.

In recent years discussions on the social aspects of stem cell research have especially focused on concepts of governance in the life sciences (Salter 2008, Gottweis 2009, Gottweis *et al.* 2009). In discussions of stem cell research in Asia, concepts of governance used to understand socio-political processes of change in Europe are widely applied to an Asian context. But such understandings of China may be premature. After all, the formulation of European concepts of governance has grown out of detailed and substantial research in a European context (*cf.* Foucault 1978, 1991). There is no reason for Asian societies not to have developed diverging notions of governance. This double special issue, then, is an appeal for readers to consider the Euro-American and high-income country origin of many of the analytical concepts we use, including that of governance and bioethics.

Bioethics regulation is often seen as crucial to the practice of stem cell research. Yet, the increasingly similar looking sets of national guidelines for stem cell research in different countries yield diverging research practices. In the special issue, we proceed from the idea that the rationales for establishing, interpreting and implementing regulation of hESR vary under different circumstances. Thus, in developing countries the advancement of science, including the shaping of research regulation, has a different weight on the national agenda, and evaluation of the progress of scientific research is measured with a different yardstick depending on the political climate and research environment of a country. Moreover, research institutions have diverging cultural, legal and political histories, so that the regulatory tools take on different shapes, varying from formal guidelines and legislation to soft guidelines and social control, depending on the institutional settings they play a role in. The aim of the double special issue, then, is to stimulate discussion on the informal research cultures, social conventions and traditions that are crucial to the way in which stem cell research (including fetal stem cells and somatic stem cells) is evolving in Asia. In brief, in the special issue we try to address themes and discussions crucial to the social organization of stem cell research, and the socio-political embedding of formal regulation.

Using examples from India, Mainland China, Japan, South Korea, Taiwan and Israel, the special issue shows that formal regulation of stem cell research is not adequately understood outside the socio-economic and political embedding of the regulation. Comparing research conditions in countries that differ in their financial capacity, level of science development, and politico-religious outlook, the double special issue shows that research regulation takes shape through a great variety of informal bioethical practices and social institutions, including religion, politics, social movements and the state. From an international, comparative point of view, the regulation of stem cell research is shown to be influenced by a constellation of factors, including the availability of research facilities, the need for attracting foreign investments and companies, the wish to maintain a clean reputation, and policies for promoting national interests, but also the social and political desire to keep the peace in society, the wish to root regulation on controversial subjects in public opinion, and the religious and cultural belief in doing what is "right."

In large developing countries, such as China and India, the questions of research funding for stem cell research, healthcare targets and the donation of embryos, fetuses and oocytes must take into account different considerations from those that apply in affluent welfare societies. This is due partly to the diverging histories of science and medical institutions, partly to different methods of regulating ethical behavior, ranging from soft socio-economic checks and controls to political and legal sanctions, and partly to the existence of different views on what socio-cultural and economic costs can and should be paid for scientific undertakings and public health projects. But crucial may be the different constellation of choices policy-makers, researchers and patients face in countries where the resources to fund science and healthcare institutions are severely restricted. International guidelines for stem cell research were set up in and for countries with particular institutional infrastructures and socio-economic provisions. Where these infrastructures are absent or inadequate, the interaction of high-tech research, socio-economic setting and unstable regulatory environment entails ethical issues of a particular nature: in such societies debates usually focus on socio-economic inequality, political (mis-) representation and competition, in addition to and intertwined with issues concerning the bioethics of using embryos, eggs and fetuses in the tissue economies of stem cell research. How problems related to the embedding of stem cell research in society play out differently in high- and low-income societies will become clear in this double special issue.

Margaret Sleeboom-Faulkner

References

Foucault, M., 1978. *The history of sexuality*, Volume 1: an introduction. Translated by Robert Hurley. New York: Random House.

Foucault, M., 1991[1979]. Governmentality. *In*: G. Burchell, C. Gordon and P. Miller, eds. *The Foucault effect*. Chicago IL: University of Chicago Press, 87–104.

Gottweis, H., 2009. Editorial: biopolitics in Asia. *New Genetics and Society*, 28 (3), 201–204.

Gottweis, H., Salter, B., and Waldby, C., 2009. *The global politics of human stem cell science: regenerative medicine in transition*. London: Palgrave.

Salter, B., 2008. Governing stem cell science in China and India: emerging economies and the global politics of innovation. *New Genetics and Society*, 27 (2), 145–159.

Sleeboom-Faulkner, M., 2007. Social-science perspectives on bioethics: predictive genetic testing (PGT) in Asia. *Journal of Bioethical Inquiry*, 4 (3), 197–206.

Sleeboom-Faulkner, M., 2010. *Frameworks of choice: predictive and genetic testing in Asia*. Amsterdam: University of Amsterdam Press.

The proliferation of stem cell therapies in post-Mao China: problematizing ethical regulation

Priscilla Song

Department of Anthropology, Washington University, St. Louis, USA

Thousands of foreign patients have sought experimental stem cell therapies in China since 2001. Despite critical scrutiny from scientific experts and tightening guidelines on the conduct of translational medicine, stem cell clinics have continued to proliferate in contemporary China. This article delves beyond regulatory exteriors to provide an ethnographic account of why unauthorized stem cell clinics targeting foreign clients have flourished under "socialism with Chinese characteristics." As the former emphasis on preventive care during Mao's era of collectivism has given way to a market-driven pursuit of high-tech interventions, changes in the political economy of healthcare have transformed China's urban medical system into a laboratory for entrepreneurial tactics. This article traces how medical entrepreneurs operate within and beyond the socialist market economy by co-opting public hospital facilities for private gain and capitalizing on the hope and hype over stem cell research to promote dubious procedures. Rather than producing biopolitical modes of governance, formal regulation in China often invites enterprising tactics and hybrid practices that ultimately remake the boundaries between public and private, as well as ethical and unethical.

Introduction

The notion of contemporary China as the "morally bankrupt 'Wild East' of biology" (Dennis 2002, p. 335) has become a trite phrase overused by Western journalists and vigorously countered by Chinese scholars and government officials. Citing scandals over poisoned toothpaste and tainted milk powder or rampant piracy of movies and software, foreign observers have bemoaned the lack of regulatory controls in the rapidly transforming People's Republic. Meanwhile, Chinese officials have emphasized tightening regulations and touted severe penalties for corrupt regulators such as the 2007 execution of Zheng Xiaoyu, the former director of China's State Food and Drug Administration.

In this article, I analyze the proliferation of Chinese stem cell clinics catering to foreign patients in order to problematize the notion of ethical regulation in post-Mao China. I focus on the lived experience of regulatory policies to question how state power, individual agency, and the pursuit of health intersect on the floors of hospital wards in urban China. Despite critical scrutiny from scientific experts and tightening guidelines regulating the conduct of stem cell research and experimental treatments, thousands of patients from over 100 countries have sought stem cell therapies in China since 2001. From Bangladesh and Belgium to the United States and the United Arab Emirates, people suffering from neurological disorders have entrusted their bodies to medical entrepreneurs in China offering "tomorrow's treatments today."

The ambiguous political status of these border-crossing stem cell patients complicates the linkages between governance and life posited by theorists of biopolitics. While Foucault's (1978) foundational work highlighted the central role of the state in managing populations, more recent interpretations have emphasized the self-optimization of individual bodies predicated on notions of risk (Rabinow 1996, Rose 2007). Contributors to the September 2009 issue of *New Genetics and Society* have called for a revaluation of these European and American-based formulations of biopolitics in light of the rapid development of life sciences in Asia. Gottweis (2009, p. 202) and colleagues suggest the emergence of a distinctively Asian form of biopolitics that hinges upon strong state support for biotechnologies, "patterns of bad governance that ignore Western standards of human rights and ethics," and the rise of "bionationalism." Ong and Chen (2010) and their collaborators have continued the critical scrutiny of how nationalist mobilizations have intersected with emerging biotechnologies in various Asian milieus. Although these ethnographic case studies demonstrate the variety of biotech policies and projects in China (Chen 2009, Greenhalgh 2009, Chen 2010, Sung 2010), India (Glasner 2009, Sunder Rajan 2010), Japan (Sleeboom-Faulkner 2010), Singapore (Waldby 2009, Ong 2010, Thompson 2010), South Korea (Gottweis and Kim 2009, Thompson 2010), Taiwan (Liu 2010), and Vietnam (Wahlberg 2009), taken as a whole they revive attention to the effects of state power on optimizing the lives of citizen populations. But in the case of US patients seeking stem cell therapies in China, stringent regulations at home have encouraged them to look beyond their own national borders for alternatives, rather than submitting docilely to local grids of power. These "medical tourists" and "biotech pilgrims" (Song 2010) travel outside the jurisdictions of their home countries yet do not fall neatly within the regulatory regimes of receiving countries. Although many have been written off as incurable by the American medical establishment, they have found refuge as valued clients in the VIP wards of Chinese public hospitals. Their transnational experiences point us beyond biopolitical modes of governance targeting citizen-patients to hybrid practices emerging in the interstices of regulatory differences.

I have been tracking the development of stem cell and other experimental cell-based therapies on the ground in China since 2004. The analysis in this article draws on a larger research project that entailed 24 months of multi-sited ethnographic fieldwork at Chinese stem cell clinics, content analysis of websites and media reports, as well as interviews with patients, caregivers, biotech entrepreneurs, and medical personnel. In this article, I focus on the activities of Shenzhen Beike Biotechnology Company,[1] which the prestigious scientific journal *Nature* dubbed "China's most prominent stem-cell therapy company" (Cyranoski 2009, 147). The company has received laudatory attention from media outlets around the world (e.g. Einhorn 2006, PressTV 2007, Cairns Post 2009, Mirror 2009). Beike has also been the focus of critical scrutiny by scientists and clinicians and was featured in *New Genetics and Society* as a case study illustrating an alternative mode of governance in translational stem cell research (Chen 2009). Based primarily on interviews with company representatives, Chen suggests that Beike's controversial inversion of the conventional "bench to bedside" model of translational medicine may no longer be viable with new regulations on the clinical application of medical technology (e.g. PRC Ministry of Health 2009). I probe beneath these regulatory exteriors to provide a deeper historical and ethnographic analysis of Beike's practices that complicates our understanding of legal and ethical regulation.

In this article, I set the stage for my analysis by first situating the Beike case study in the context of stem cell geopolitics. I then examine how medical entrepreneurs in China operate within and beyond the socialist market economy by co-opting public hospital facilities for private gain. In the final section, I demonstrate how these entrepreneurs capitalize on the hope and hype over stem cell research to leverage ethics itself as a marketing tool. Rather than halting dubious practices, legal and ethical regulations in China often channel entrepreneurial tactics in new and unexpected directions that may ironically produce contradictory results.

Lucrative ventures: the Shenzhen Beike Biotechnology Company

Stem cell clinics in China have capitalized on the patchwork of uneven policies regarding stem cell research in various countries to attract lucrative transnational clients, as clinics in India have done (Bharadwaj and Glasner 2009). Beike Biotechnology Company, for example, was established in 2005 by Sean Hu, a Chinese molecular biologist who had trained abroad in Sweden and Canada and returned home to set up a new biotech venture in the Shenzhen Hi-Tech Industrial Park. While the previous generation of Chinese scholars sought to remain in their adopted countries (particularly in the aftermath of the Tiananmen Square crackdown), Hu was part of a growing wave of returnees who sensed greater opportunities back home.

The city of Shenzhen offered particular advantages for biotech entrepreneurs such as Hu. Located just across the border from Hong Kong, Shenzhen was designated China's first "Special Economic Zone" (SEZ) in 1979 under the "opening and reform" policies of Chinese leader Deng Xiaoping. A key experiment in stimulating the country's development after a decade of stagnation during the Cultural Revolution, SEZs such as Shenzhen were designed to attract foreign investment particularly from "patriotic overseas Chinese and compatriots from Hong Kong" (Wu 1985, p. 133) with the goal of promoting industrial development and facilitating exports. Unlike major urban centers nearby such as Guangzhou, Shenzhen was exempt from provincial regulations. The Shenzhen government thus had significant leeway to implement policies encouraging economic development.

While headquartered in Shenzhen, Beike Biotech operated as a distributed network linking laboratories and hospitals in different areas of the country. CEO Sean Hu recruited scientists and clinicians working on stem cell culture and transplantation techniques such as Yang Bo, a neurosurgeon at the First Affiliated Hospital of Zhengzhou University in Henan Province, who began experimenting with stem cell therapies for patients with neurological disorders in 2001. Hu provided the catalyst for transforming these clinicians' research into a commercial enterprise.

From its inception, Beike pursued the lucrative potential in treating foreign clients. Hu partnered with foreign entrepreneurs operating in China such as Jonathan Hakim, an American expatriate who spoke Chinese fluently and had worked as an information technology and healthcare consultant in Hong Kong, Beijing, and Qingdao. Capitalizing on the potential of the Internet for direct-to-consumer marketing of new medical treatments, Hakim created a website called "China Stem Cell News" (http://www.stemcellschina.com/) which aggregated English-language reports on Chinese stem cell research and posted accounts of patients who had undergone stem cell treatment in China. The website initially featured a "Who is Who" section that profiled various stem cell researchers and treatment centers throughout the country, reflecting Hakim's interest in working with multiple purveyors of stem cell therapies. Although nominally a "news" source that purported to provide objective and comprehensive information, the China Stem Cell News website ultimately became a patient recruitment tool for a single company: Beike. Not surprisingly, the organization of the website reflected this transformation, replacing the researcher profiles with narrative-style "patient experiences" documenting the increasing numbers of people who underwent Beike's stem cell treatment. Hakim launched the partnership with a "news" flash on 27 September 2005 announcing "Beike to Treat Foreign Patients" (China Stem Cell News 2005a). Striking the pose of disinterested observers, the self-declared (but unidentified) "China Stem Cell Staff" noted that they had "witnessed some treatments, before during and after" which resulted in "impressive improvements." To further reassure potential Western clients, the article declared that "one member of the Stem Cell China News group is a doctor from the US and has been to the facilities and feels they are up to standard along with the doctors" (China Stem Cell News

2005a). The unnamed doctor was Hakim's father, a US-based urologist. The article instructed interested patients to click on a link that generated an email to Hakim, who had agreed to coordinate the logistics of the transnational medical procedure on behalf of Beike.

The first foreign patient received Beike's stem cell treatment in November 2005. Bob was a retired sea captain from Texas suffering from amyotrophic lateral sclerosis. I had first met him seven months earlier in Beijing, where he had tried a different experimental surgery in the hopes of halting the disease that was steadily ravaging his muscles and compromising his ability to breathe. In exchange for serving as a reference for other interested clients and keeping a journal of his experiences which the company would publish on the China Stem Cell News website, Bob was offered a free course of the stem cell injections at the Nanshan District People's Hospital in Shenzhen. The "free" treatment still entailed significant expense for the retiree and his wife, as they had to pay for their own roundtrip airfare between Texas and Hong Kong, hospital fees, medical tests, housing expenses, and meals. Beike arranged a room for Bob in the VIP ward on the 20th floor of the hospital and provided five stem cell treatments derived from umbilical cord blood which would be injected over the course of a month into his spinal cord fluid via a lumbar puncture. These cells were flown in on the day of each procedure from Yang's laboratory in Zhenzhou and then injected by a Nanshan neurosurgeon. As Bob summarized his experience in his diary, "I am the very first foreign patient and the procedure in general is very experimental yet, so there was never a guarantee, but I admit to being a bit disappointed so far with my own results." His diary was posted online together with an assessment from the China Stem Cell News staff: "Did not notice differences on his own but his friends say he is walking better. Slight increase in hand strength on both arms as tested by grip meter" (China Stem Cell News 2005b).

Since Bob's initial therapy at Nanshan Hospital in 2005, Beike claims that it has treated over 5,000 foreign patients. Positioning itself as "the most important Group in stem-cells treatment in China" (Beike 2007a), Beike's marketing brochure for European clients declares:

> Beike's greatest strength and the key factor which differentiates us from other research initiatives is that we specialize in clinical applications. We know there are a lot of patients in countries around the world who could have a better quality of life and even extend their lives with the technology available ... but don't have the chance because of politics, religion and bureaucracy. Our goal is to help those people. We take the most advanced biotechnological research in the world, specifically stem cell therapy, and apply it clinically at a rapid pace. (Beike 2007b)

Although critics have lambasted Beike for marketing unproven therapies to desperate patients, company representatives suggest that the real problem lies in extraneous red tape preventing people from getting the care they deserve. This framing deflects questions about the scientific challenges involved in translating laboratory results into useful clinical applications, shifting attention instead to the political debates stymieing patients' access to new treatments.

"Wearing a red hat": the unintended effects of regulation

To understand why public Chinese hospitals such as Nanshan have collaborated with Beike to treat foreign patients with experimental stem cell therapies, we need to situate this development in the context of China's changing healthcare system. Once heralded internationally as an example of universal preventive care during Mao's era of collectivism, the Chinese healthcare system has faced tremendous pressure from conflicting state policies seeking to generate profits while preserving access to healthcare over the past 30 years (Blumenthal and Hsiao 2005). The central government significantly reduced public funding of state-owned health facilities beginning in the 1980s, following policies that proved successful in increasing the profitability and efficiency of agricultural and industrial sectors. But in seeking to ensure access to basic healthcare, the Ministry of Health also continued to enforce below-cost charges on a wide range of routine medical services. As a frustrated staff internist at an elite Beijing hospital complained to me, an appointment with him cost the same as using a public toilet.

These features of Chinese healthcare policy reflect the peculiar political economy of what Mao's successor Deng Xiaoping branded "socialism with Chinese characteristics": a volatile combination of decentralization coupled with continued state control over strategic sectors. Although the central government maintained strict price controls on what it considered essential healthcare, it permitted hospitals to set their own fees for new medical services. Developing advanced medical technologies thus became one of the few legitimate means of generating revenues.

This trend has blossomed in the profit-driven priorities of "healthcare with Chinese characteristics,"[2] emphasizing high-tech medical services at corresponding higher prices. Hospitals across the country have created elite wards offering a range of high-tech services catering to wealthy consumers – a particularly lucrative strategy for Nanshan Hospital, given its proximity to Hong Kong. Second-tier hospitals such as Nanshan have also turned to external sources to generate revenue. By reinventing themselves as real estate brokers, these hospitals "lease departments" [*chuzu keshi* 出租科室] or "contract out wards" [*waibao keshi* 外包科室] to medical entrepreneurs. While the PRC State Council (1994) has declared such conduct illegal, savvy medical entrepreneurs such as Beike's CEO Sean Hu circumvent these regulations by partnering with a network of medical universities and local governments. These hospitals thus gain institutional credibility and legal recognition as "academic partners" of a lucrative joint venture stimulating local economies.

Beike Biotech's partnership with second-tier public hospitals entails paying "cooperation" fees to house its clients in VIP rooms, utilize nursing services, and collaborate with local physicians. The company essentially conducts its own health-related activities within the public hospital – from recruiting patients and performing stem cell injections to setting fees and collecting payments – with little or no oversight from the contracting hospital. This model of operating "a hospital within a hospital" [*yuan zhong yuan* 院中院] constitutes an alternative tactic often described in Chinese business circles as "wearing a red hat" [*dai hong maozi* 戴红帽子]. As sociologist David Wank discovered in his study of Chinese entrepreneurs in the southern coastal city Xiamen, another designated Special Economic Zone, private companies often sought legal registration as public enterprises as a cover for their business activities. These affiliations between entrepreneurs and local bureaucracies blurred the boundaries between private and public ownership. Partly stemming from the socialist valorization of public property and status, the phenomenon of "wearing a red hat" was also an eminently practical, profit-oriented tactic that enabled entrepreneurs to take advantage of tax breaks, acquire institutional legitimacy, and obtain other benefits. The public agency partnering with the private company also benefited from these business ties, as entrepreneurs paid to use the "often underutilized or idle assets of the public units such as real estate and machinery" (Wank 2001, p. 79).

Local crackdowns on hospital operations have little effect on the operations of a distributed network such as Beike. Because they are merely using space within a partner hospital, these biotech entrepreneurs can easily move to a new location should any problems arise. As a Beike client from Florida described in an online journal documenting his treatment in China: "The Dr's here in Shenzhen don't really want to do the surgical injection on me, and I want it done. Qingdao is where I am having surgery where they will cut in to the back of my neck and inject the stem cells directly in to the injury site." (Allen 2006).

As Jerry's entry suggests, when faced with problems or challenges at one site, Beike representatives could easily make arrangements with a more cooperative site to satisfy the demands of their customers. In Jerry's case, doctors at Nanshan Hospital, who had been contracted by Beike to perform the stem cell injections in patients' private rooms either intravenously through the blood stream or into the spinal fluid via a lumbar puncture, balked at performing the more risky laminectomy which would involve exposing his spinal cord under general anesthesia in the operating room. Jerry thus travelled over 1,600 kilometers to a hospital in another province willing to perform the procedure. As his experience illustrates, while professional qualms of medical personnel or oversight by hospital administrators or even regional health bureaus may regulate unauthorized practices at one site, they have the unintended consequence of shifting questionable activities to another node in Beike's diffuse network.

Capitalizing on ethics: stem cell confusions and conflations

If legal regulations have little effect in governing Beike's overall operations, what about ethical guidelines? In this section, I demonstrate how ethics itself has become co-opted as a marketing tool in Beike's arsenal of business practices rather than serving as a normative guide to regulate dubious practices. Beike's patient-consumers cite the "ethical" nature of the company's cells as an important factor in their decision to become clients of the company. Beike achieves this feat by exploiting the controversy over embryonic versus adult stem cells.

All stem cells are undifferentiated cells which can give rise to various other types of cells, but embryonic stem cells theoretically have the most potential for clinical application since they are capable of becoming any other somatic (bodily) cell type. The scientific challenge that embryonic stem cell researchers have faced, however, is controlling the differentiation process in order to produce the specific desired cell type. "Adult" stem cells, such as hematopoietic and neural stem cells, specialize in the generation of a smaller range of cells usually limited to the tissue type in which the adult stem cell is located. Some researchers have claimed that these adult progenitor cells can produce the differentiated cells of another tissue type (Bjornson *et al.* 1999, Lagasse *et al.* 2000, Krause *et al.* 2001). Because research with adult stem cells does not require the destruction of human embryos, political and religious conservatives have seized upon this form of research as morally desirable even though intense debate remains in the scientific community over whether and to what extent these adult stem cells can in fact "transdifferentiate" (Anderson *et al.* 2001, Abkowitz 2002, Schwartz 2006).

Beike offers patients with neurological disorders injections of hematopoietic (blood-forming) stem cells delivered into the spinal fluid via a lumbar puncture or intravenously into the bloodstream. These adult stem cells are present in small quantities in umbilical cord blood as well as bone marrow, and they give rise to red and white blood cells, platelets, and other blood and immune cells. Beike's sales pitch to prospective clients emphasizes the moral differences between embryonic and adult stem cells while leaving out questions about the physiological mechanisms by which their proffered injections counter the neurological problems experienced by patients.

Jason travelled from Calgary to undergo stem cell therapy at one of Beike's affiliated hospitals in Hangzhou in March of 2009, 16 years after he was first diagnosed with multiple sclerosis. In his public blog hosted by the China Stem Cell News website, the Canadian explained the superior nature of the cells he would be receiving from the company:

> The stem cells that I will be receiving are "ethically friendly" as I like to put it. Although China certainly didn't have the same ethical problems with doing research on embryonic stem cells as we had in North America, what their research found out was that the embryonic stem cells don't really work. They are, you might say, too adaptable. Apparently, as I understand it, when they tested them on animals, the animals grew really strange, awful, monstrous tumours with hairs and teeth and eyes and the like! They had no control over what kind of cell the embryonic stem cell would turn into. However, umbilical or plaacental [sic] stem cells (also called adult stem cells I believe) work very well, and are what I will be receiving, along with stem cells

harvested from my own bone marrow. They are also, of course, ethically friendly. I find this fascinating as it makes the whole furor over stem cells rather moot! (Jason 2009)

In this Canadian patient's understanding, Beike's treatment offers the perfect alignment of ethics and efficacy: the unethical use of embryos is an uncontrollable, dangerous practice that resulted in "monstrous" consequences, while the "ethically friendly" umbilical cord and bone marrow stem cells conveniently "work very well." Jason's explanation, as well as Beike's own promotional literature, offers notably little detail on how these cells might actually function once inside his body.

Marketing the "ethically friendly" nature of their treatment on the cellular level enables Beike executives to circumvent larger questions both about the scientific challenges involved in translational research and the moral quandaries of selling unproven therapies to patients. Beike's biotech entrepreneurs sidestep these discussions by advertising bone marrow and umbilical cord blood injections as a "safe" form of "stem cell therapy." In fact, hematopoietic stem cells have been used clinically for nearly 40 years in the form of bone marrow transplantation to treat leukemia, but specifically as a way to repopulate blood cells following radiation or chemotherapy to destroy cancerous cells (Thomas *et al.* 1975). Beike's savvy marketing touting the safety of hematopoietic stem cells conveniently elides the lack of definitive evidence for whether these cells can produce the new neurons so ardently desired by those suffering from neurodegenerative conditions.

Furthermore, bone marrow and umbilical cord blood contain only a small percentage of hematopoietic stem cells. Although Beike claims that each "stem cell" injection it offers contains approximately 10 million cells (Beike 2007c), the specific details about its methods of cell purification are scant in its marketing materials and it has yet to publish any peer-reviewed scientific articles detailing its procedures. This is not a trivial question, as scientists have not yet developed consistent methods to purify the notoriously elusive hematopoietic stem cells found in bone marrow and umbilical cord blood.

The vast majority of so-called "stem cell therapies" being marketed to patients leverage the clinical history and ethical appeal of adult stem cells while capitalizing on the hope generated by embryonic stem cell research. Without the magical words "stem cell" attached to the experimental treatment, I doubt whether consumers would be so eager to sign up for Beike's services. But Beike's "stem cell" therapies may in fact be physiologically equivalent to injecting blood cells into patients' spinal columns – blood transfusions, in other words. Even if we accept Beike's (rather dubious) claims that it is providing over 10 million hematopoietic stem cells with each injection, these cells may just differentiate into red and white blood cells – if they even reach the site of injury or survive at all.

Conclusion: beyond regulatory exteriors

I have sought to move beyond regulatory exteriors in order to provide a deeper ethnographic analysis of why unauthorized stem cell clinics targeting foreign clients have flourished under "socialism with Chinese characteristics." Social analysts have pointed to the "governance vacuum" and "lack of governance clarity" (Salter 2008, p. 153) as driving forces in the development of stem cell research in Asia. Glasner (2009, p. 288), for example, has argued that lax regulations and the lack of a statutory framework for enforcing guidelines have enabled "maverick scientists" in India to develop stem cell therapies in a "liminal space ... without bureaucratically defined ethical approval." The implication is that "more ethics" (i.e. establishing stricter guidelines) will enable better governance of these unruly practices.

But as Jacob and Riles (2007) have noted in their analysis of the "bureaucracies of virtue," the institutionalization of ethical guidelines produces new (and often unintended) forms of agency and personhood. While Jacob, Riles, and their colleagues have focused on practices of informed consent, my ethnographic research on stem cell therapies suggests that formal regulation in China often invites enterprising tactics that constitute new relationships between clinician-entrepreneurs and patient-consumers. Beike's medical entrepreneurs operate within and beyond the socialist market economy by co-opting public hospital facilities for private gain and capitalizing on the hope and hype over stem cell research to leverage ethics itself as a marketing tool to attract lucrative foreign clients. These hybrid practices ultimately problematize the role of ethical regulation in governing transnational regimes of bioscience.

Acknowledgements

This research was supported by a US National Science Foundation Graduate Research Fellowship. I would like to thank the patients, caregivers, medical personnel, and entrepreneurs who shared their experiences with me. I am grateful to Margaret Sleeboom-Faulkner for inviting me to present the ideas discussed in this article at the 2008 symposium on "The social regulation of stem cell research" at the University of Sussex and the 2010 "International science and bioethics collaborations in Asia" colloquium at the University of Cambridge. I would also like to thank my colleagues at Washington University and the anonymous reviewers for *New Genetics and Society* for their helpful feedback.

Notes

1. Anthropologists have traditionally disguised the identities of people, institutions, and even places we analyze in our published work. But in an era when our informants post their own accounts online and our field sites are visited by journalists, anonymity has become increasingly untenable. Although I have continued to protect the identities of people who shared their experiences with me in confidence, I have chosen to cite the actual names of people and institutions in cases where I obtained information about them from publicly available sources such as blogs, websites, media reports, and corporate news releases. This commitment to openness is particularly important for companies marketing experimental treatments to vulnerable patients. Rather than leaving the task to journalists and press release writers, scholars should also analyze these practices publicly so that prospective families thinking of undergoing the procedures can make a more informed decision about their medical choices.

2. I invoke this phrase to underscore the contradictory nature of Chinese efforts to reform healthcare since the 1980s. In recent years, high level officials such as Gao Qiang, former Party Secretary of

the Chinese Ministry of Health, have publicly acknowledged the failures of these earlier market-based reforms and emphasized providing for the public good as the essence of "the road to health development under socialism with Chinese characteristics" (Xinhua News Agency 2008).

References

Abkowitz, J., 2002. Can human hematopoietic stem cells become skin, gut, or liver cells? *New England Journal of Medicine*, 346 (10), 770–772.

Allen, G., 2006. Welcome to my life journey: Jerry's personal site [online]. Available from: http://www.mylifejourney.net/letters.htm [Accessed 26 October 2009].

Anderson, D.J., Gage, F.H., and Weissman, I.L., 2001. Can stem cells cross lineage boundaries? *Nature Medicine*, 7, 393–395.

Beike, 2007a. What is Beike Europe [online]. Available from: http://www.beike.ch/index.php?option=com_frontpage&Itemid=1 [Accessed 15 May 2007].

Beike, 2007b. Beike Group [online]. Available from: http://www.beike.ch/index.php?option=com_content&task=view&id=5&Itemid=5 [Accessed 15 May 2007].

Beike, 2007c. Treatment cost [online]. Available from: http://www.beike.ch/index.php?option=com_content&task=view&id=2&Itemid=2 [Accessed 15 May 2007].

Bharadwaj, A. and Glasner, P., 2009. *Local cells, global science: the rise of stem cell research in India*. London: Routledge.

Bjornson, C.R., *et al.*, 1999. Turning brain into blood: a hematopoietic fate adopted by adult neural stem cells in vivo. *Science*, 283, 534–537.

Blumenthal, D. and Hsiao, W., 2005. Privatization and its discontents: the evolving Chinese health care system. *New England Journal of Medicine*, 353 (11), 1165–1170.

Cairns Post, 2009. Improvements stem from cell therapy. *Cairns Post*, 19 April [online]. Available from: http://www.cairns.com.au/article/2009/04/18/38681_local-news.html [Accessed 28 February 2011].

Chen, H., 2009. Stem cell governance in China: from bench to bedside? *New Genetics and Society*, 28 (3), 267–282.

Chen, N., 2010. Feeding the nation: Chinese biotechnology and genetically modified foods. *In*: A. Ong and N. Chen, eds. *Asian biotech: ethics and communities of fate*. Durham, NC: Duke University Press, 81–92.

China Stem Cell News, 2005a. Beike to treat foreign patients [online]. Available from: http://www.stemcellschina.com/index.php?option=com_content&task=view&id=1&Itemid=43 [Accessed 1 November 2005].

China Stem Cell News, 2005b. Beike – Bob Naugle. Patient experience – ALS [online]. Available from: http://www.stemcellschina.com/index.php/en/patient-experiences/als-patients/89-beike-bob-naugle [Accessed 28 February 2011].

Cyranoski, D., 2009. Stem-cell therapy faces more scrutiny in China: but regulations remain unclear for companies that supply treatments. *Nature*, 459, 146–147.

Dennis, C., 2002. China: stem cells rise in the East. *Nature*, 419, 334–336.

Einhorn, B., 2006. Blinding science: China's race to innovate. *Business Week*, 31 March [online]. Available from: http://www.businessweek.com/globalbiz/content/mar2006/gb20060331_921612.htm [Accessed 28 February 2011].

Foucault, M., 1978. *The history of sexuality, Volume 1: an introduction*. Translated by R. Hurley. New York: Random House.

Glasner, P., 2009. Cellular division: social and political complexity in Indian stem cell research. *New Genetics and Society*, 28 (3), 283–296.

Gottweis, H., 2009. Editorial: biopolitics in Asia. *New Genetics and Society*, 28 (3), 201–204.

Gottweis, H. and Kim, B., 2009. Bionationalism, stem cells, BSE, and Web 2.0 in South Korea: toward the reconfiguration of biopolitics. *New Genetics and Society*, 28 (3), 223–239.

Greenhalgh, S., 2009. The Chinese biopolitical: facing the twenty-first century. *New Genetics and Society*, 28 (3), 205–222.

Jacob, M.A. and Riles, A., 2007. The new bureaucracies of virtue: introduction. *PoLAR: Political and Legal Anthropology Review*, 30 (2), 181–191.

Jason, 2009. Jason's MS blog: getting Beike's stem cell treatments at Hangzhou Xiaoshan Hospital [online]. Available from: http://stemcellschina.com/blog/JasonN/ [Accessed 28 February 2011].

Krause, D.S., *et al.*, 2001. Multi-organ, multi-lineage engraftment by a single bone marrow-derived stem cell. *Cell*, 105, 369–377.

Lagasse, E., *et al.*, 2000. Purified hematopoietic stem cells can differentiate into hepatocytes in vivo. *Nature Medicine*, 6, 1229–1234.

Liu, J., 2010. Making Taiwanese (stem cells): identity, genetics, and hybridity. *In*: A. Ong and N. Chen, eds. *Asian biotech: ethics and communities of fate*. Durham, NC: Duke University Press, 239–262.

Mirror, 2009. Stem cell miracle gives gift of sight to Dakota: Ulster girl has pioneering treatment at Chinese clinic. *The Mirror* (UK), 5 (March) p. 11.

Ong, A., 2010. Lifelines: the ethics of blood banking for family and beyond. *In*: A. Ong and N. Chen, eds. *Asian biotech: ethics and communities of fate*. Durham, NC: Duke University Press, 190–214.

Ong, A. and Chen, N., 2010. *Asian biotech: ethics and communities of fate*. Durham, NC: Duke University Press.

PRC Ministry of Health, 2009. Yiliao jishu linchuang yingyong guanli banfa 医疗技术临床应用管理办法; [Regulations on the clinical use of biomedical technologies] [online]. Available from: http://www.moh.gov.cn/publicfiles/business/htmlfiles/mohyzs/s3585/200903/39511.htm [Accessed 28 February 2011].

PRC State Council, 1994. Yiliao jigou guanli tiaoli 医疗机构管理条例 [Regulation of medical institutions] [online]. Available from: http://www.gov.cn/banshi/2005-08/01/content_19113.htm. [Accessed 28 February 2011].

PressTV, 2007. A revolution in Chinese stem cell technology [online]. Available from: http://www.presstv.ir/textonly/detail.aspx?id=30720 [Accessed 26 October 2009].

Rabinow, P., ed., 1996. Artificiality and enlightenment: from socio-biology to biosociality. *In: Essays on the anthropology of reason*. Princeton, NJ: Princeton University Press, 91–111.

Rose, N., 2007. *The politics of life itself: biomedicine, power, and subjectivity in the twenty-first century*. Princeton, NJ: Princeton University Press.

Salter, B., 2008. Governing stem cell science in China and India: emerging economies and the global politics of innovation. *New Genetics and Society*, 27 (2), 145–159.

Schwartz, R.S., 2006. The politics and promise of stem cell research. *New England Journal of Medicine*, 355 (12), 1189–1191.

Sleeboom-Faulkner, M., 2010. Embryo controversies and governing stem cell research in Japan: how to regulate regenerative futures. *In*: A. Ong and N. Chen, eds. *Asian biotech: ethics and communities of fate*. Durham, NC: Duke University Press, 215–236.

Song, P., 2010. Biotech pilgrims and the transnational quest for stem cell cures. *Medical Anthropology*, 29 (4), 384–402.

Sunder Rajan, K., 2010. The experimental machinery of global clinical trials: case studies from India. *In*: A. Ong and N. Chen, eds. *Asian biotech: ethics and communities of fate*. Durham, NC: Duke University Press, 55–80.

Sung, W., 2010. Chinese DNA: genomics and bionation. *In*: A. Ong and N. Chen, eds. *Asian biotech: ethics and communities of fate*. Durham, NC: Duke University Press, 263–292.

Thomas, E.D., *et al.*, 1975. Bone-marrow transplantation. *New England Journal of Medicine*, 292 (16), 832–843.

Thompson, C., 2010. Asian regeneration? Nationalism and internationalism in stem cell research in South Korea and Singapore. *In*: A. Ong and N. Chen, eds. *Asian biotech: ethics and communities of fate*. Durham, NC: Duke University Press, 95–117.

Wahlberg, A., 2009. Bodies and populations: life optimization in Vietnam. *New Genetics and Society*, 28 (3), 241–251.

Waldby, C., 2009. Biobanking in Singapore: post-developmental state, experimental population. *New Genetics and Society*, 28 (3), 253–265.

Wank, D.L., 2001. *Commodifying communism: business, trust, and politics in a Chinese city*. Cambridge: Cambridge University Press.

Wu, C.T., 1985. China's special economic zones: five years later. *Asian Journal of Public Administration*, 7 (2), 127–143.

Xinhua News Agency, 2008. Gao Qiang: Zhongguo tese weisheng fazhan daolu jujue mangmu yinjin guowai moshi 高强：中国特色卫生发展道路拒绝盲目引进国外模式 [Gao Qiang: health development road with Chinese characteristics cannot blindly introduce foreign models] [online]. Available from: http://gov.people.com.cn/GB/46728/113521/113525/6752508.html [Accessed 28 February 2011].

Recruiter-patients as ambiguous symbols of health: bionetworking and stem cell therapy in India

Prasanna Kumar Patra[a] and Margaret Sleeboom-Faulkner[b]

[a]Department of Anthropology, Utkal University, Bhubaneswar, India; [b]Department of Anthropology, University of Sussex, Falmer, UK

Healthcare service providing centers in India offer contentious stem cell-based therapies to patients for an array of medical conditions. Among strategies these centers adopt to recruit new patients from local, regional and global spheres, the most prominent is the use of "recruiter-patients." Recruiter-patients are a group of patients who either have already received or are in the process of receiving the therapy and, importantly, are used by service providers as mediums or tools to attract desperate yet novice therapy seeking patients to the ambit of the stem cell therapy enterprise. This article is based on a multi-sited ethnographic study at stem cell-based therapy providing centers in different parts of India between July 2008 and June 2009. Using the concepts of "bionetworking" and "ambiguous symbols," this article explores how recruiter-patients are used by service providers as tools for the recruitment of new patients and why they are effective.

Introduction

Stem cell therapy (SCT) is emerging globally, including in India, as a novel and promising treatment for several medical conditions such as spinal cord injury, diabetic ulcer and myocardial infarction for which conventional medicine is considered to be ineffective (Wainwright *et al.* 2006, Williams *et al.* 2008). Wealthy and "desperate" patients from across local and global spheres constitute the main target groups for this therapy (Lindvall and Hyun 2009, Patra and Sleeboom-Faulkner 2010). Competition among therapy providers has become increasingly fierce, even though the efficacies of the therapies are now questioned internationally among scientists (Duncan *et al.* 2008, Hyun *et al.* 2008, Lander *et al.* 2008). One issue of sociological relevance is what mechanisms exist for the recruitment of clients. This article researches one of the strategies used by some service providers to draw clients into the ambit of the treatment. They adopt a strategy whereby patients who either have received treatment or are undergoing treatment at several service providing centers play an important role as "recruiter-patients" to influence potential patients who are desperately looking for treatment avenues. These recruiter-patients are used as mediums or tools to influence potential clients/ patients in various ways, including personal meetings with new patients or relatives in clinics, telephonic advice, and web-based advertisements in the form of testimonials.

This article aims to show how recruiter-patients are used to attract desperate patients. First, it provides empirical evidence on the workings of recruiter-patients as lucrative tools; second, it shows how recruiter-patients are used to enrich the bionetworks of private therapy providers in hospitals; and, third, the analysis in this article shows how the multiple social functionality of the image of patients is exploited by strategically turning them into ambiguous symbols, thereby violating the trust of potential patients in stem cell therapies.

Methodology

Data for this study was collected using qualitative anthropological fieldwork methods, including participant observations and semi-structured interviews. The study was conducted at various stem cell therapy providing centers and research institutions located in different parts of India. These locations were selected on the basis of their reputation as leading stem cell research and/or therapeutic service providing centers by using patient narratives, media reports and web searches.

Based on their mode of service provision, there are three kinds of SCT providers in India, namely, public sector, private sector and independent practitioners. Semi-structured interviews were conducted with medical care givers, stem cell researchers, treatment-seeking patients and their accompanying family members or relatives at three public sector hospitals, three private sector hospital-cum-stem cell research institutes and three locations where independent practitioners make experimental stem cell therapy (ESCT) provision available. The first author has interviewed, among others, seven patients and their relatives, five stem cell scientists, six medical doctors, eight middle-level stem cell researchers, three project heads and five ethics committee members of Institutional Review Boards (IRBs) at the various institutes.

Participant observations were conducted at two stem cell-based service providing centers in Delhi and Chennai. The first author spent at least six hours a day for a period of one week at each place observing the day-to-day activities of the research staff, medical care givers, visits of patients and relatives to the clinic, negotiations between the service provider and service seeker about the care and the interaction that they have in the hospital situation. Both the service provider and seeker had prior knowledge of the presence of a social science researcher interested in the treatment. It must be made clear here that the first author did not always have access to all interactions between service providers and seekers.

Fieldwork-based primary data gathering for this study was carried out for a period of three months, within a period of one year stretching between July 2008 and June 2009. Several follow-up telephonic interviews and email communications with key informants and interviewees are also part of this study. The research upon which this study is based has been through ethical review at the universities of Sussex and Cambridge. We have used pseudonyms to maintain confidentiality and to protect the identity of research participants, but the names of individuals and institutions well known in the public sphere we have not altered. Interviews in the field were conducted in English and in the local language, such as Hindi, Oriya and Bengali. Interview materials quoted in this text are presented verbatim for interviews conducted in English. Translated interviews from local languages are indicated in the text.

Stem cell therapy and patient recruitment in India

Over the last decade India has emerged as one of the preferred locations for stem cell-related research and as a site for experimental stem cell-based intervention activities. It has become possible due to, on the one hand, proportionally greater investment by the state in medical biotechnology research and development (Salter *et al.* 2007), a state of stem cell "governance vacuum" (Sleeboom-Faulkner and Patra 2008) and a lack of authority for regulators to enforce policies (Pandya 2008). On the other hand, India has benefited from the policy decisions and ethical dilemmas over embryonic stem cell research in the USA (e.g. NIH's moratorium on public funding for stem cell research in 2001) and stringent regulation on the clinical application of adult stem cell therapies in the West (Kulkarni 2008, Salter 2008). Government policies on stem cell science in India have been very supportive of programs that aim at promoting both basic and translational research in view of its potential application (Sharma 2006). Among policy issues, public–private partnership in basic and translational research in stem cell science is given importance, which signifies an atmosphere of renewed vigor, flow of capital and strengthening of capabilities. There are many such initiatives in India among academic institutes, hospitals and industries in the field of stem cell research and therapy. In India, stem cell application or therapy services are on the way to becoming a common practice – with many tertiary level hospitals and healthcare centers entering into stem cell research and/or clinical application as part of their service provision.

Service providers have varied motivations and interests in making stem cell therapy available to their patients/clients depending on their institutional alliances, locations and patient recruitment strategies. For instance, the main motivation behind service providers in publicly funded tertiary level hospitals is to make the therapy available to a maximum number of patients at an affordable price, whereas privately funded healthcare centers view it as a commercial enterprise and target a client patient population that is needy, desperate and wealthy. In this article our main focus is on therapy providing centers that have alliances with private sector healthcare centers. These centers offer service providers a maximum dynamism in terms of infrastructural growth and patient recruitment, while providing potential links across local and global spheres to exploit the variations in local conditions and national regulatory mechanisms. The main focus of this article centers on service providers based in private sector institutions.

Bionetworking

In this article, by using the concept of "bionetworking," we have attempted to describe the strategies that stem cell therapy service providers, especially those based in the private sector, employ in order to recruit patients from local and global spheres. Bionetworking, in the context of our study, denotes a form of connecting up with key individuals involved in research and healthcare organizations who take advantage of the unequal socio-economic and regulatory contexts in which stem cell research takes place and therapy is provided.

The concept of "bionetworking," on the one hand, refers to the ways in which stem cell therapy providers make use of local, national and global differences in regulatory, political, and economic circumstances and healthcare provision, and is used to capture informal forms of social and entrepreneurial liaisons within them. It recognizes that the "business of biomedicine" (involving patients and biomaterials) is negotiated by life scientists, science managers, medical professionals and patients. Thus, bionetworking concerns their strategic decision-making based on knowledge and perceptions of regional and global inequities, and differences in regulatory regimes and research cultures (Sleeboom-Faulkner 2010). On the other hand, the concept links together institutional complexities covering both private and public means, semi-underground activities in small hospitals and healthcare hubs, and comprises the initiatives of individual physicians in hospitals and university researchers by revealing the functional connectivity between medical institutions and the kinds of therapies they provide: the activity of bionetworking makes use of the ambiguity of formulations and the gaps in the regulation of stem cell research, its poor implementation, and the unmet needs of patients both at home in India and abroad.

Recruiter-patients

In the field of business, sellers are known to use agents who pretend to be enthusiastic clients with the aim of promoting a particular product. As will be shown, this kind of strategy is also used in the field of biomedical technology. For, in stem cell therapy, service providing centers use patients as agents to influence and attract new patients. We term these patients "recruiter-patients." In the context of stem cell therapy in India, recruiter-patients either have received or are in the process of receiving stem cell therapy. This phenomenon is associated with "non-standard" medical practice, mostly conducted covertly or in the guise of officially authorized clinical trials.

Recruiter-patients are used as tools by the service providers in various ways – in web-based advertisements with video clips showing patients' testimonials of the improvement in their medical conditions, by allowing desperate and new patients and their relatives to meet a "cured" patient in person and in arranging telephonic talks between recruiter-patients and clients. Three conditions characterize the development and the use of recruiter-patients. First, stem cell therapy enterprise is largely provided covertly, so that patient recruitment is generally conducted behind closed doors. Second, a situation of fierce competition among service providers in private sector hospitals/clinics in India has led to unscrupulous methods to attract a maximal number of patients; and third, the regulatory apparatus of the state is unable to monitor these stem cell therapy enterprises.

Recruiter-patients as ambiguous symbols

In this article we use the concept of "ambiguous symbols" to shed light on the social relationship between recruiter-patients, therapy providers and potential patients. Ambiguous symbols can be meaningful in different ways to different stakeholders and they can be employed to disguise actual practices. In this case, the concept of "recruiter-patient" is used to symbolize successful treatment. In the case of recruiter-patients, the "regained" health of the recruiter-patient as a symbol of health signifies positive medical experience. Providers use the so-called newly found health of the cured patient as a symbol for successful therapy. Potentially, this performance forms a lucrative source of income for the service provider, while potential patients are unaware of the unevidenced nature of the experimental therapies the recruiter-patients disguise. Although recruiter-patients embody the symbolism of "cured patients," to service providers they symbolize the promise of potential patients. The ambiguous symbolism of the recruiter-patient, then, serves the continuity of an exchange characterized by inequality, dependence, and manipulated potentialities of health and profit.

In practice, this ambiguity is revealed only rarely. One instance is when the Public Relation Officer of a stem cell service providing hospital in Chennai commented on the use of "old-patients" – those who have already received the therapy – as tools for the recruitment of new clients:

> To view some patients as mere "recruitment tools" or "instruments" is something that undermines their self-esteem and the fact that they are autonomous, intelligent and people with human values. It is undignified to categorize them as such. Rather I will call their services as something very humane, something with higher virtue. I believe some of them, not all, do it as part of their gratitude towards the hospital and more towards the therapy as a source of hope and solution to their problem. (Translation by PKP)

In this perspective the service provider views a patient's gratitude towards the hospital as a form of obligation. Some patients may truly feel indebted to the hospital as the treatment they receive they believe to be unavailable elsewhere. They feel it as their duty to return their debt and also to help other patients. For instance, one spinal cord injury patient from Rajasthan, who received adult and embryonic stem cell therapy at different places in India, explained:

> I feel particularly obliged to inform other patients in need of help about the availability of stem cell therapy at such and such places. I feel this as part of my duty in belonging to a particular kind of disease group. I do not like others to face the same kind of anxiety and desperation that I faced when I was looking for a therapy. Moreover, I feel obliged to the hospital for whatever improvement I find after three years of life with a wheelchair. I too have a duty towards other patients. (Translation by PKP)

From the perspective of a patient who has received therapy for an ailment that has no success with conventional modes of treatment, developing a sense of gratitude is not uncommon. Service providers exploit the gratitude of patients and attempt to institutionalize it as part of their client-recruitment strategy.

Other cases concern not the performance of ex-patients, but the charade of healthy individuals. A relative of a spinal cord injury patient, who has closely observed and interacted with several stem cell therapy service providing centers in India, made the following observation:

> Several clinics and hospitals that are providing stem cell therapy do use some patients as agents in order to influence desperate patients looking for treatment avenues. Sometimes, they are even fakes. Members of their office staff pretend to be cured patients. They do *nautanki* [pretend] as if they are real patients who have benefited from a therapeutic service and do influence others to take the therapy. Of course this happens only when there is a telephonic interaction. The whole exercise of seeking prior information from old-patients or interacting with them through telephonic interaction is almost always forged and is stage-managed by service providers. (Translation by PKP)

The reach of impersonal interactions, such as telephonic conversations between recruiter-patients and clients, is limited. But other kinds of impersonal interactions, such as web-based patient testimonials have a wider reach, as more and more desperate and terminally ill patients from resource-rich countries and wealthy patients from resource-constrained countries have Internet access. Recent studies (Lau *et al.* 2008, Regenberg *et al.* 2009) show how direct-to-consumer advertising via the Internet is likely to play an important role in an "early market" where patients are seeking and accessing putative stem cell therapies. A web-based patient testimony by Amanda Boxtel, an American patient who has received contentious embryonic stem cell therapy in a private clinic in New Delhi comes across as very persuasive. She writes:

I am compelled to share my experiences with the world. After fifteen and a half years of being in a wheelchair as a T11-12 complete spinal cord injury and two months of HESC treatment, my toes are moving; my bladder and bowels are beginning to function again; I have increased muscle power in my legs; and hope is now a part of my vocabulary! (Boxtel 12 September 2009)

Elsewhere she writes:

Any new bodily improvements that I have experienced since the first day of treatment in India on June 25, 2007 I attribute to the Human Embryonic Stem Cells. There is no other explanation. A positive attitude, prayer, diet, or alternative therapies never brought life and restored function into my legs. My body's awakening is proof in itself. For this reason, I know I haven't been injected with a placebo or apple juice. (Boxtel 12 September 2009)

It is difficult to determine whether such testimonials genuinely portray patients' experiences of improvement in their medical condition and gratitude towards service providers. But there is no doubt that such testimonials are compelling in nature and content. Stem cell providers, then, exploit the symbolism of "cured patients" to attract new patients. Although it is not clear if "the cured patient" is a grateful patient, or a person paid to act as one, the symbolism of "the cured patient" is crucial to the connection between all involved.

Stem cell tourism and the role of recruiter-patients

The phenomenon of "stem cell tourism" and the emerging role of recruiter-patients are closely related. Stem cell tourism is a new form of medical travel (Lindvall and Hyun 2009) across local, regional and global locations driven by hope and hype. As the flow of patients across countries in search of stem cell-based treatment is growing, so are the concerns over baseless claims, adverse medical effects and unethical means in patient recruitment (Kiatpongsan and Sipp 2009, Lindvall and Hyun 2009, Patra and Sleeboom-Faulkner 2009).

In the Indian context we categorize three types of service providers according to their drive for service provision and their institutional embedding within Indian healthcare: the public sector, the private sector and individual practitioners. These various service providers employ diverging networks for the promotion of research into stem cell science and for patient recruitment. The kind of infrastructure that private centers develop around stem cell services, the kind of advertisement they circulate and the kind of patients they recruit for SCT services were indicative of their bioethical stance. Personnel in the public hospitals, financed by the state and representing official government policy, view the emergence and scope of stem cell research and therapy as a social enterprise that has potential to transform the economic and healthcare needs of the nation and do not tend to use recruiter-patients. For the private sector healthcare providers, stem cell research and therapy constitute a commercial enterprise in a time of healthcare privatization and the state's encouragement of public–private partnership in techno-scientific research. Individual practitioners consider stem cell research and therapy as an opportunity for earning money, and gaining professional experience and fame, while targeting growing numbers of middle class patients searching for healthcare outside the public sector.

The role of recruiter-patients is more prominent in the private sector and among individual practitioners in comparison to the public sector. Patient recruitment requires a well-defined strategy that varies across service providing centers and hospitals depending on their size, infrastructure and networking tactics. The use of patients to attract new clients is an integral part of the private service provider's scheme. A public relations officer of a multi-specialty private hospital in Chennai, which claims to have provided stem cell-based therapy to over 400 patients in the last two years for various medical conditions, explains the rationale of using recruiter-patients:

> People will come to you only when they see the results for themselves and they are convinced about it. They want to see it before they believe it. Or at least they want to listen first hand. You know, they have to spend so much money, therefore they should have a chance to see for themselves and listen to the experiences of patients who have benefited from the treatment. For that reason we arrange meetings with patients or provide their contact details so that they can directly interact. For us the patients who have received good results from the treatment are our best advocates. You can say they are our ambassadors.

The views of patients and their relatives about the role of recruiter-patients varies, usually depending on the therapy provider they are associated with. Some patients and relatives believe that recruiter-patients have played an important role in their decision to go for stem cell therapy. They feel that the first hand narrative of the recruiter-patient helped them to take an informed decision about the risks and benefits involved, about the quality of service and about what to expect from the treatment. One patient, who had recently received several doses of embryonic stem cell therapy at a private clinic based in New Delhi, narrated the following:

> We came to know about this clinic in Delhi from a patient who had received stem cell-based therapy here for spinal cord injury. Upon our request, the clinic provided his contact address to us. The clinic even arranged a meeting between the cured patient and us (family members). After seeing the patient's improvements, his self-confidence and after listening to his narratives we decided to receive the therapy. His narratives and experiences were very convincing. (Translation by PKP)

Another patient had a different experience. Mr V believed that the contact addresses and names of patients provided by the clinic/hospital for pre-service interactions were fake, and that they constituted manipulative acts by the clinics concerned. He claimed that recruiter-patients work as agents for private providers and that their main job is to attract as many patients as possible into the ambit of therapeutics:

I urge people not to fall prey to the trap that these hospitals are adopting. To my utter shock, the doctor and the whole LL hospital system are into fraudulent activities. They use "old patients" and their false testimonials to influence clients. When I asked for contact numbers of some patients, I was given two contact numbers by the public relations officer of the stem cell department at the hospital. The two patients I contacted over the phone had a very high opinion about the treatment results and hospital facilities. But they showed one or the other pretext to avoid a personal meeting with me. Later on I found out that the numbers provided belong to the staff of the same hospital and the patients were not real but fake. I felt cheated. (Translation by PKP)

Private hospitals involved in stem cell therapy services try to maximize patient intake by the strategic use of recruiter-patients: their symbolic value as cured patients is used to entice patients to undergo unverified therapies. But when the health symbolism of recruiter-patients is questioned, the meaning of healthcare provision in general becomes problematic.

Recruiter-patients as ambiguous symbols of health

This section is based on two cases related to a particular hospital called LL Hospital in Chennai. The first case is based on a web-based narrative by a patient who had received adult stem cell therapy for his spinal cord injury and the second case is based on the first author's meeting with the same hospital personnel. The cases illustrate how stem cell therapy service providing centers in the private sector use the symbolism of cured patients and forge the role of recruiter-patients strategically as part of their bionetwork.

LL Hospital is a group of hospitals based in Chennai, a city in southern India, which claims to have provided stem cell-based therapies successfully to nearly 400 patients over the last two years for an array of medical conditions, including spinal cord injury, myocardial infarction and diabetic ulcer. LL Hospital claims that nearly 30% of its clients constitute patients from abroad, especially from the USA, Canada, Australia, Spain, Pakistan and Sri Lanka. The multi-specialty center of the hospital has branches all over the city of Chennai and within the state of Tamilnadu. It draws patients from these branch hospitals through referral and on a recommendation basis using a "hub-and-spoke" model.

Case 1

Mr Patel, a spinal cord injury patient from Gujarat, contacted LL Hospital for possible stem cell therapy after he had been unsuccessfully treated for the ailment elsewhere. He came to know about the hospital from a newspaper article and subsequently from the hospital's website. Desperately, he wrote an email to the head of the stem cell section at LL Hospital, Dr R, for guidance. Dr R advised him to speak to two patients who had been successfully treated for similar injury at LL Hospital. Upon his contact with both the patients, Mr Patel was given positive feedback about the treatment and the hospital. Mr Patel was then influenced by the feedback and decided to take the therapy at LL Hospital. But after a while, he became suspicious of their communication, including that with the coordinator of the hospitals who managed the treatments and one of the patients with whom he had interacted earlier. Eventually, he became convinced that the voices of the coordinator and the patients were one and the same and that he had been scammed. In his blog on the Internet the patient made the following statement about the incident:

> A while back I spoke to Mr. SR who is a coordinator of the stem cell department in Life-line hospital. Something was very fishy; the voices of Mr. SV and Mr. SR seemed very similar. So I went to the website http://www.stemcell-india.com/ and checked the *Contact us* section http://www.stemcell-india.com/contact.htm. I was so hurt to see the Mr. SR's number on this page and Mr. SV's number on the above email were one and the same. (Taken from the web-blog of Mr Birju Patel, dated 8 February 2007)

Not surprisingly, the magic attraction of the recruiter-patient disappeared in the mind of the disillusioned patient.

Case 2

The first author independently visited LL Hospital in Chennai and met with the coordinator and physician-in-charge of the stem cell therapy department. Upon request to meet patients who have had successful stem cell transplantation, the author was provided with two contact numbers, one of which gave no response. The other was found to be a recruiter-patient who gave very positive views about the treatment and the hospital's medical services. But the patient did not want to meet personally, as he lived far away from Chennai city. After cross-checking the contact number, it was found to be identical to the number of a member of the stem cell department of LL Hospital. The identity of the patient had been forged and the whole episode appeared to be stage-managed.

The cases show a similar storyline in which the authenticity of recruiter-patients is disputed by service seekers when they discover that some service providers are pretending and acting as cured patients. When the pretence of the service provider is revealed, stem cell therapy in itself becomes disputable, with has consequences for the acknowledgement of the integrity of stem cell research in general.

Conclusion

With the growing public expectations of stem cell therapy and the widening access to global information flows, recruiter-patients based at the local and global spheres of stem cell therapy providing centers have come to play a crucial role in clinical stem cell applications. The proliferation of unverified stem cell-based medical treatments has complicated the decision-making of patients and their relatives with the increased use of recruiter-patients.

Recruiter-patients have become a means through which bionetworking activities are executed by service providers: they exploit relations of dependency and financial and health uncertainties around the globe. Recruiter-patients link together service providers, patient groups and their families, and stem cell therapy technologies across local and global spheres of practice. In bionetworking, private providers strategically mobilize recruiter-patients as human symbolic baits to attract patients to controversial experimental stem cell therapies.

The symbolism of "cured patients" is crucial to the decision-making of potential patients that have little means to verify either the scientific value of the therapy or the veracity of the recruiter-patient, but much to gain from effective treatment. When recruiter-patients are found to be fake, the symbolism of "cured patients" loses its meaning, but also the value of stem cell therapy is doubted. It is not just the faith in healthcare providers that is at stake here, but the future of regenerative medicine could well suffer from the disillusionment of these patients. For patients it was the recruiter-patient that embodied the "proof of the pudding" that could not be provided by scientific evidence.

Acknowledgements

The research for this article was mode possible through the Netherlands Organisation of Science (NWO-050-32-530) and ESRC (RES-350-27-0002; RES-062-23-0215).

References

Boxtel, A., 2009 [Title not available] [online]. Available from: http://www.rhcfoundation.org/amanda. htm [Accessed 12 September 2009].

Duncan, I.D., *et al.*, 2008. Stem cell therapy in multiple sclerosis: promise and controversy. *Multiple Sclerosis*, 14, 541–546.

Hyun, I., *et al.*, 2008. New ISSCR guidelines underscore major principles for responsible translational stem cell research. *Cell Stem Cell*, 3, 607–609.

Kiatpongsan, S. and Sipp, D., 2009. Monitoring and regulating offshore stem cell treatments. *Science*, 323, 1564–1565.

Kulkarni, 2008. Asia to dominate adult stem cell commercialization. *BioSpectrum*, 14 October 2008 [online]. Available from: http://biospectrumindia.ciol.com/content/Bio/Business/10810147.asp [Accessed 13 May 2011].

Lander, B., *et al.*, 2008. Harnessing stem cells for health needs in India. *Cell Stem Cell*, 3, 11–15.

Lau, D., *et al.*, 2008. Stem cell clinics online: the direct-to-consumer portrayal of stem cell medicine. *Cell Stem Cell*, 3, 591–594.

Lindvall, O. and Hyun, I., 2009. Medical innovation versus stem cell tourism. *Science*, 324, 1664–1665.

Pandya, S., 2008. Stem cell transplantation in India: tall claims, questionable ethics. *Indian Journal of Medical Ethics*, 5 (1), 15–17.

Patra, P.K. and Sleeboom-Faulkner, M., 2009. Bionetworking: experimental stem cell therapy and patient recruitment in India. *Anthropology and Medicine*, 16 (2), 147–163.

Patra, P.K. and Sleeboom-Faulkner, M., 2010. Bionetworking: between guidelines and practice in stem cell therapy enterprise in India. *SCRIPTed – A Journal of Law, Technology and Society*, 7 (2), 295–310.

Regenberg, A.C., *et al.*, 2009. Medicine on the fringe: stem cell-based interventions in advance of evidence. *Stem Cells*, 27, 2312–2319.

Salter, B., 2008. Governing stem cell science in China and India: emerging economies and the global politics of innovation. *New Genetics and Society*, 27 (2), 145–159.

Salter, B., *et al.*, 2007. Stem cell science in India: emerging economies and the politics of globalization. *Regenerative Medicine*, 2 (1), 75–89.

Sharma, A., 2006. Stem cell research in India: emerging scenario and policy concerns. *Asian Biotechnology and Development Review*, 8 (3), 43–53.

Sleeboom-Faulkner, M. and Patra, P.K., 2008. The bioethical vacuum: national policies on human embryonic stem cell research in India and China. *Journal of International Biotechnology Law*, 5 (6), 221–234.

Sleeboom-Faulkner, M., 2010. Contested embryonic culture in Japan-public discussion, and human embryonic stem cell research in an aging welfare society. *Medical Anthropology*, 29 (1), 44–70.

Wainwright, S.P., *et al.*, 2006. From bench to bedside? Biomedical scientists' expectations of stem cell science as a future therapy for diabetes. *Social Science and Medicine*, 63, 2052–2064.

Williams, C., *et al.*, 2008. Human embryos as boundary objects? Some reflections on the biomedical worlds of embryonic stem cells and pre-implantation genetic diagnosis. *New Genetics and Society*, 27 (1), 7–18.

Exploring appropriation of "surplus" ova and embryos in Indian IVF clinics

Jyotsna A. Gupta

University for Humanist Studies, Utrecht, The Netherlands

IVF clinics have emerged and are proliferating even in small towns of India. There is hardly any regulation or oversight regarding what happens to "surplus" ova and embryos, the potential raw material for embryonic stem cell research. India is an emerging economy where both public and private initiatives in stem cell research exist and are proliferating. There is a lack of transparency regarding the supply of stem cells required for research. Based on empirical research, the article provides insight into the practices and policy relating to the appropriation of human ova/embryos by IVF clinics and health (research) institutions. It also investigates the regulatory structures to govern procurement and ownership of ova/embryos, and whether they are likely to be adequate and effective. It concludes that the existing guidelines are not binding, lack legislative authority and adequate monitoring mechanisms, leaving the practice in IVF clinics to self-regulation. This creates a potential for exploitation of ova/embryo donors.

Introduction

Clinics providing in-vitro fertilization (IVF) have proliferated even in small towns of India. Not only Indian infertile couples are flocking to these clinics; India is a major destination for couples from abroad seeking donor eggs and surrogates to fulfill their desire for a child. IVF clinics are also the potential suppliers of ova and embryos for stem cell research. India is an emerging economy, where both public and private initiatives in stem cell research exist and are proliferating, riding on the second wave of globalization in the biomedical and information technology industry. Public–private partnerships are also being undertaken. Research in India is not only dependent on national or foreign private enterprise and capital; there is a huge investment also by the Indian government in this sector. The Department of Biotechnology has supported more than 30 programs of stem cell research so far, including the establishment of "stem cell city clusters" (UK Stem Cell Initiative 2005). It announced its intention to create a biotechnology industry that would generate US$5 billion in revenues per year and one million jobs by 2010 (Jayaraman 2005 cited in Salter *et al.* 2006). The National Task Force on Stem Cell Research was established in April 2005 to take these plans forward. Gaining and maintenance of trust through appropriate governance and account-ability structures is crucial for success and further development at a national and international level, since India has become a global center for clinical trials both for its own industry and for contract research organizations working on behalf of foreign companies (Salter *et al.* 2006, Frew *et al.* 2007, Sunder Rajan 2007). However, there is a lack of transparency regarding procurement of human ova and embryos required for research.

My focus here is on the appropriation of raw materials (e.g. ova and embryos) required either for IVF practice or for the early stage research in stem cells. I look at the clinical practice in IVF clinics to understand the process of procure-ment of ova/embryos and clients' views regarding donation. Further, I discuss regulatory structures for governing the procurement and ownership of eggs/ embryos in place, and examine other ethical issues regarding ova appropriation for IVF treatment and for stem cell research.

Research methodology and methods

Data was obtained through empirical research conducted in New Delhi and Mumbai during 2002–2004 and again in January 2009. Interviews using qualitat-ive research methods were held with (a) 28 women/couples attending two selected IVF clinics; (b) 17 IVF specialists at 10 clinics; and (c) three regulators. Only three of the 10 clinics had their own research labs. Most IVF clinics were not involved in research; the researcher did not inquire whether they had links with other research labs. Permission from and access to the couples in various stages of IVF treatment was obtained from the IVF specialists and individuals in question and the latter were interviewed while waiting for their turn to see the specialist in the clinic. The interviews were in a semi-structured open-ended format, which allowed women/couples to relate their experiences of the IVF treatment. Questions pertained to demographic details, information regarding the IVF process, their own experience of it, who should decide what happened with their reproductive material, whether they would be willing to donate their "surplus" eggs either to another couple or for research, and their use of the consent forms. Also, consent forms used by the clinics were requested, and when obtained analyzed. All interviews were fully transcribed, after which major themes were identified, and relevant excerpts selected.

Procurement of ova for research

The major source of ova for research is women undergoing infertility treatment requiring ovarian stimulation and egg retrieval. There is an enormous increase worldwide in the number of women seeking assisted reproduction including IVF. Women enrolled in IVF programs are administered fertility drugs to hyper-stimulate the ovaries to ripen (multiple) eggs. Doctors have retrieved as many as 44 eggs (normally one egg matures in every menstrual cycle). Ova and embryos are not merely a "gift of life," but also a "gift of potential knowledge to a medical researcher" (Waldby and Mitchell 2006).

Initially, the ethics of procurement of ova for research was never seen as an important issue even by bioethicists; concerns regarding the moral status of the embryo overshadowed this aspect. The media, and even the scientific journals, were "as silent on the issue as if human eggs grew on trees" (Dickenson and Alkorta Idiakez 2008, 127). Dickenson (2006, cited in Dickenson and Alkorta Idiakez 2008, 127) argues "much bioethical analysis simply ignored the way in which 'the lady vanishes' in the SCNT stem cell technologies." Few ethnographic studies deal with the procurement of eggs for research (Thompson 2005, Roberts 2007, Bharadwaj and Glasner 2009) and what qualifies an embryo to be regarded as spare (Scully and Rehman-Sutter 2006, Svendsen and Koch 2008).

After it came to light in 2005 that South Korean research led by Hwang Woo-Suk involved fabricated data and the unethical procurement of over 2,200 eggs (Kim 2008), those advocating the need for setting international standards regarding ova procurement have been increasingly vociferous; this, however, appears to be a challenging task as in different countries the regulatory frameworks, legal norms and legislation – from the rather permissive to more tolerating regimes – regarding egg donation are diverse, if they exist at all. In many countries, including Spain and the US, mainly young university students are recruited as egg donors for infertile women and paid a handsome fee ranging from US$800 to US$5,000 respectively. Apparently, Harvard university scientists are finding it difficult to persuade women to donate eggs for research, as it is illegal to pay them when eggs are used for research purposes (Dizikes 2007), whereas Spanish donors would rather donate for research than IVF, given the confidentiality impli-cations of donating gametes for reproduction (Dickenson and Alkorta Idiakez 2008).

In the UK, the Human Fertilisation and Embryology Authority (HFEA) agreed on 21 February 2007 to allow women to donate their eggs for research provided strong safeguards were in place to ensure that women were properly informed of the risks of the procedure and protected from coercion. Both altruistic donation or in conjunction with their IVF treatment are allowed, and they are eligible for discounted IVF services and compensation for actual costs incurred such as trans-portation up to £250 (HFEA 2007). The HFEA is keen to remove obstacles to donation. A public consultation on a market in gametes began in January 2011 running for three months. The results will be made available in May 2011 (Cook 2010).

Even when women are paid thousands of dollars, as in the US, for reproductive purposes, the procedure is referred to as "egg donation" to avoid the connotation of a market in human eggs (Resnick 2001). Haimes (2008 cited in Haimes and Taylor 2009, 2142) opines "there is a strong case for using the more neutral language of 'provision.'" It is difficult to strictly define the lines defining the various modes of transactions – donation, gift, altruism and commerce – in body parts and tissues. While the sale of solid organs is illegal in most countries, including India, ova, semen, blood and other body fluids and tissues do not fall under the legislation because of their regenerative quality. Also, transactions in these body parts are relatively unregulated, primarily due to the idea of individual autonomy (Dickenson and Alkorta Idiakez 2008, Gupta and Richters 2008), which, it is believed, can be taken care of through informed consent procedures. The new guidelines of the International Society for Stem Cell Research (ISSCR 2007) legitimize both reimbursement of direct expenses and financial compensation for women who supply eggs for research. They recommend that decisions about paying women for their eggs should be left to local oversight committees.

Ova appropriation in Indian IVF clinics

According to recent media reports, there are about 350 fertility clinics in India, some of which provide state-of-the-art facilities, while others in semi-urban areas function as satellite clinics. In contrast to the 1990s, with wider availability of IVF and donor eggs, in recent years Indian women even in their late 40s and 50s are seeking IVF. Women are hyper-ovulated to ripen multiple follicles. The eggs are harvested to produce the maximum number of embryos in-vitro, more than the number transferred in women. In India, doctors replace three to five embryos, especially in women above 35, or if there is a history of previous failures (two to three IVF cycles) (interview material). Because affordability of patients is low, this works out cheaper, increasing the chance of success per cycle. Most clinics run donor-recipient egg-sharing programs. Both women are said to benefit from this egg-sharing method. Usually, poor patients exercise the option to donate their eggs in exchange for their treatment costs being shared either by the receiving couple or by the clinic.

To the researcher's remark during interviews that university students in the US were selling their eggs to pay for their education, one patient remarked "the government should reduce the fees, so that students would not have to sell their eggs," while another iterated "according to our tradition it is not proper to sell eggs." An IVF specialist mentioned that it was difficult to find (non-patient) women willing to donate their eggs, because the process is painstaking. It requires a woman to undergo a series of tests and take injections for 12 days to hyper-stimulate the ovaries, after which the eggs are harvested. Few women want to go through this for nothing. Another reason mentioned by a fertility specialist was that egg extraction involves trans-vaginal ultrasound for egg harvesting. "You wouldn't have that kind of girls [as in the US and Spain] coming forward, you know, to take 20 injections. Because most of the work we do is internal, doing a trans-vaginal ultrasound for an unmarried Indian girl and egg pick-up wouldn't be acceptable" (interview Dr J).

However, recently the media report a new trend that fertility specialists are receiving requests for egg donation from young elite Indian college students and single working women – women who want to earn quick money to maintain their expensive lifestyles (Sharma 2010). Also, the recent economic downturn resulting in job losses seems to be driving some housewives to resort to egg selling to balance family budgets and lifestyles (interview Dr A). This phenomenon needs further research.

Consent forms and obtaining consent

Most clinics claim to use a consent form which women and their husbands under-going assisted reproduction procedures must sign before treatment can begin. In some cases the consent form is part of an information booklet. As one service provider said: "Actually, ours is like a booklet. So, when they go through it, they have to sign the entire booklet" (interview Dr I). Most clauses on the form mention (1) techniques to be used; (2) that the risks and failures at various points of the procedure have been explained to clients; and (3) an achieved preg-nancy is not guaranteed. Remarkably, the same form is also used to register an agreement between the different parties (client/donor/hospital) involved regarding the use of "leftover" eggs; there is no separate form for cryopreservation or use of "leftover" or donor eggs/embryos. In practice, this means that unless clients sign the consent form treatment cannot begin, and once they have signed it they have also relinquished their rights to their own leftover eggs/embryos.

I tried to procure sample consent forms from IVF specialists. While some were cautious and reluctant to oblige, making up some excuse or other, some others did make the form available to me. Here are a few samples of the clauses on the consent forms of some of the leading clinics in Delhi and Mumbai regarding use of "left-over" eggs/embryos:

> We understand that extra oocytes/embryos will be dealt with by the clinic at their own discretion for cryofreezing/donation/scientific research. (Kamala Polyclinic & Nursing Home, Mumbai)

> We are willing to give away the immature eggs for research in case they do not mature in vitro after 48 hours of incubation in appropriate media.
> We are willing to give the unfertilized eggs for research, which fail to fertilize in vitro following IVF or ICSI. (INKUS IVF Centre, Mumbai)

> We both understand that the disposal of unused oocytes/embryos shall be at the discretion of the IVF unit. (Sir Ganga Ram Hospital, New Delhi)

As one service provider put it:

> We have a consent form, no legal agreement. We have no separate form for consent regarding cryopreservation. The same consent form is used for donation. (Dr F)

In 2003 the following notice appeared on the wall of the IVF unit of a renowned private hospital in New Delhi.

Note:

Patients are hereby informed to make the payment for cryopreservation done on due date.

Cryopreservation of embryos is valid for six months from the date of cryopreservation which can be renewed on payment of renewal charges within the last month of Validity Period. Failure of which authorizes laboratory to treat the embryos as discarded.

Charges are as follows:

Cryopreservation charge: 15,000 Rupees. (valid for first six months)

Renewal charges: 3,000 Rupees. (valid for next six months from last month of first validity period)

Thus, patients pay for storage of their embryos. If they fail to pay, after two reminders the clinic may use the embryos for donation to other couples or for research. "Discard" may mean any of the following: destroy, sell, use for research, etc.; effectively it means a transfer of custody of embryos from the "donors" to the IVF clinic on the expiry of a fixed time period. This was confirmed by one of the IVF specialists at this hospital.

It is clear from the above examples that the majority of women undergoing IVF are unwittingly being asked to donate or relinquish ownership over their "spare" or "supernumerary" eggs/embryos without realizing that these are a potentially valuable resource having a "biovalue" (Waldby and Mitchell 2006) or "biocapital" (Sunder Rajan 2007).

I asked couples undergoing treatment whether they had signed a consent form, regarding use of leftover eggs/embryos. Many remembered signing something, but not exactly what was written on the form.

On the second or third day we signed something; even today. We believe them (doctors) and have confidence in them. So, we don't read the terms and conditions, or say "delete this or that, and only then we'll sign." (PKG, husband)

Another (male) replied:

Yes, we signed. It's a printed form; so, you can't change anything.

I don't know what they do with the extra eggs. Generally they say they discard them. Naturally, they can't keep so many containers; otherwise the hospital would be full of them. (P, female)

I asked women/couples undergoing IVF whether they would be prepared to donate their eggs.

Mr S: My wife wouldn't be.
Researcher (R): Would you consider selling them?
Mr S: No. If there is a choice we would prefer donating them, but not selling.

R: In the US, female students are selling their eggs.
Mr S: We wouldn't do that.
R: And what about donating them for research?
Mr S: Sure.
(Mr JNS, husband of woman undergoing IVF)

I asked whether they expected that their consent would be taken, if their leftover eggs were donated to some other woman/couple, or used for research.

(1) BK (husband): See, when we make offerings [money] in the temple, the priest may drink away the money. We don't check it out.
R: Would you allow your spare eggs to be used for research?
SK (wife): No problem, if it is for the good of others.
(Couple undergoing IVF)

(2) R: Would you consider donating the extra eggs?
AP: Eight eggs have been retrieved. I would like to keep the extra embryos for a second pregnancy. After that I would be happy to donate …We don't expect payment, because we earn enough.
(Woman who had undergone IVF, six weeks pregnant)

(3) R: Would you donate embryos for research?
MG: I was asked to donate and donated 8–9 cryopreserved embryos, because I already have twins … I don't mind if anything can be done for science.
(Dr MG, gynecologist, who had given birth to twins after IVF)

(4) R: Would you donate the extra eggs for research?
V: Yes, why not? As long as the hospital does not use them commercially. If I donate, the hospital has to donate also. If not, I object to it.
(Woman undergoing IVF)

From the interview material it emerged that most women/couples were under great physiological and psychological pressure. They were too preoccupied with the IVF treatment and their desire for a child and had given little thought to what would be done with their eggs/embryos once they had achieved their goal. Often they did not ask, neither were they informed how many eggs had been harvested or the number of embryos created. If there were sufficient eggs available for their own use (later attempts if needed), many couples felt "the extra eggs have no value for us." Also, they did not desire payment for the "donated" eggs. Having gone through so much trouble themselves, helping other couples in a similar predicament or helping science to come up with solutions to infertility were reasons often-mentioned by women/couples undergoing IVF to donate their eggs. The (high) costs for cryopreservation was a reason for letting it lapse. Patients did not have much idea about what "research" entails.

Few patients had read the consent forms carefully. In practice, it emerges that the primary function of consent forms is to protect the practitioner from liability, not to protect the patient from injury or abuse. Also, more importantly, they serve to transfer custody – contractual "ownership" – of embryos from patients to IVF clinics, either actively or by default.

Dr M, at the National Institute for Research in Reproductive Health, Mumbai (a public sector institute), then President of the Indian Society of Assisted Reproduction was very critical of some of the practitioners in her field:

> In India, if you go to the best of clinics, you'll find that most of them don't bother to take consent. They think they are doing humanitarian work to suit themselves, which is not what I practice; I practice science the way it should be practiced ... Dr X tells the patient: "Maybe I will transfer only three of your embryos." The patient asks "what will you do with the rest of my embryos?" Dr X says: "I'll throw them out. I'm not going to preserve them." Whether she preserves them, or gives them to someone else, this is her own business, not ours. We would have three times the practice if we were to give the eggs away, because we have a large IVF program ... We do cryopreservation, we also do donor-recipient cycles and I have currently a stem cell research program, where frozen embryos with the consent of donor are used. Our center is registered with NIH [National Institute of Health] in America.

Several IVF practitioners I interviewed told me they followed guidelines prepared by the Federation of Obstetric and Gynaecological Societies of India, the European Society of Human Reproduction and Embryology or the American Fertility Society, although these claims cannot be verified.

Regulation and governance in India

Government policies regarding stem cell research are shaped differently in different national regimes. Unlike the law and practice in countries such the UK, US, Belgium, Israel and Singapore, which are well regulated, India does not have an official policy in place yet, although some guidelines (DBT-ICMR 2007) in this regard exist.

The first set of guidelines were prepared by the Indian Council of Medical Research and the National Academy of Medical Sciences (India), posted on their website, circulated among practitioners, and finally published in 2004. These guidelines were further sharpened in 2007 (DBT-ICMR 2007) to address both ethical and scientific concerns to encourage responsible practices in the area of stem cell research and therapy. They include a special section on the procurement of gametes, blastocysts or somatic cells for the generation of hES cell lines. Only surplus, spare and supernumerary eggs may be used for research after informed consent is obtained from both spouses. These can be collected only in registered Assisted Reproductive (IVF) Clinics. Clauses and sub-clauses in section 11 are relevant here. According to them:

> Consent for donation of supernumerary embryos should be obtained from each donor at least 24 hours in advance and not at the time of donation itself. Even people who have given prior indication of their intent to donate blastocysts that remain unutilized after clinical care should give fresh informed consent at the time of donation of the embryo for establishment of hES cell line. Donors should be informed that they

retain the right to withdraw consent until the blastocysts are actually used in cell line derivation (Clause 11.2).

There should be no commodification of human oocyte, human sperm or human embryo by way of payment or services, except for reimbursement of reasonable expenses incurred by the person (amount to be decided by IC-SCRT/IEC. Similarly, no payments should be made for donation of somatic cells for use in SCNT except for reimbursement of direct expenses incurred for attending the clinic (Clause 11.3).

Women should be informed about potential hazards and complications that are related to the hormonal induction process and be provided appropriate healthcare in case of complications arising from the procedure (Clause 11.4).

The attending physician responsible for the infertility treatment and the investigator deriving or proposing to use hES cells preferably should not be the same person. To facilitate autonomous choice, decisions related to the creation of embryos for infertility treatment should be free of the influence of investigators who propose to derive or use hES cells in research (Clause 11.5).

In the context of donation of gametes or blastocysts for hES cell research or therapy, the informed consent process, should at a minimum, provide the following information: A statement that the blastocysts or gametes will be used to derive hES cells/cell lines for research purposes (Clause 11.6a).

. . .

A statement that neither consenting nor refusing to donate embryos for research will affect the quality of present or future medical care provided to potential donors (Clause 11.6j).

Apart from an institutional ethical committee, a nodal body for review and monitoring, the National Apex Committee for Stem Cell Research and Therapy (NAC-SCRT) was proposed. All institutions and investigators, both public and private, carrying out research on human stem cells should be registered with the NAC-SCRT through the Institutional Committee for Stem Cell Research and Therapy (IC-SCRT) (Clauses 4.0 and 4.1).

The DBT/ICMR 2007 guidelines do not have legislative authority and the ad hoc character of the proposed monitoring and enforcement agency make it no more than a paper tiger. This leaves clinicians and researchers free to practice some sort of "self-regulation." Most people (including some providers of IVF) are skeptical of guidelines having the intended effect on the practice in clinics and research centers, particularly in the private sector (interview material). "Guidelines are at best good practice and, at worst, just scraps of paper," according to a lawyer in the Supreme Court of India specializing in corporate law and regulatory issues in biotechnology. Moreover, existing guidelines cannot be enforced on private organizations that do not receive government funding (Mudur 2005). Private clinics make use of this regulatory vacuum to do as they like and justify their activities in the name of "helping mankind" and putting India on the global stem cells research map. An often cited case is that of Dr Geeta Shroff, an obstetrician/gynecologist who specialized in IVF in the early 1990s, but is not doing IVF any more. I interviewed her in 2007. Dr Shroff began her research in stem cells in 2000 at Nu Tech Mediworld in New Delhi, a registered genetic center which started as a fertility clinic. She claims that she created a stem cell line with only one "leftover" embryo. The conditions under which the eggs were procured, whether consent from the women involved was obtained, and its validity, remain unanswered questions, considering she has not made these issues transparent even to the ICMR (interview regulator).

Jayaraman (2001 cited in Bharadwaj and Glasner 2009) confirms that India is being increasingly seen as an embryo surplus nation. In an environment which at the moment is almost free for all, and with the rapidly increasing fertility interventions for both the local and international market, and with evidence of the growing fertility tourism, India is likely to become a stem cell "hub." Also, "the Church in Western countries perceives using embryos to extract stem cells as murder. This, in conjunction with lax regulations on such research, has given India an obvious edge" (Pandeya 2007 cited in Bharadwaj and Glasner 2009, p. 104). The influence of the Church on the perceived status of the embryo and its influence on stem cell research policy varies in different countries. In India, abortion is widely practiced as a family planning measure and also within pre-natal management of pregnancy by all religious groups (Gupta 2010). There have been hardly any debates on the moral status of the embryo, even within the Christian and Muslim communities, traditionally perceived as opposed to abortion.

In the wake of setting up the hESC line research at Reliance Life Sciences Laboratory and the National Centre of Biological Sciences in 2001 and its associated publicity, the government announced a "crackdown" on the trade to counter the international view of India as "an embryo surplus" nation (Salter *et al.* 2006). The claims of self-regulation made by IVF practitioners, that they follow international guidelines (those of the American Fertility Society and HFEA, UK) in this regard, and lack of transparency and monitoring of this highly lucrative burgeoning fertility industry, leave the question unanswered whether the ova/ embryos were procured ethically.

Discussion

In many countries ova donation for research purposes lacks any governance framework whatsoever, at either national or international level. It may be clear from the interviews above that in Indian IVF clinics there is little regulation and even lesser oversight regarding what happens to "surplus" ova/embryos. Women/couples undergoing IVF procedures often neither ask nor are told how many eggs have been harvested or the number of embryos resulting from the procedure (interview material). Thus, the potential for exploitation is high. As Waldby (2008, p. 20) argues, "the existing exploitative procurement networks for reproductive oocytes could readily be used to obtain research oocytes as well, if no measures are taken to prevent this."

Also, one may ask whether the practice of reduction of treatment costs for ova/embryo donors is acceptable and does not imply an indirect inducement for agreeing to give away their supernumerary ova/embryos. Most of the interviewed women undergoing IVF procedures were not keen to sell their eggs; they would rather donate. Traditional cultural ideas and socialization encouraging altruistic donation seemed to influence their decision (Gupta and Richters 2008). Ova and embryos, because of their highly minuscule nature, unlike semen or other body parts and tissues, are a less visible or tangible entity. Perhaps this, too, plays a role in the fact that women sign away and transfer their rights to their use to other women/couples undergoing infertility treatments and IVF clinics. Bharadwaj's ethnography of Indian IVF clinics reveals that the informed consent process could be problematic, but service providers and research scientists believe that, if counseled properly, donors see nothing wrong in giving up "spare" embryos for research. Therefore, the crux of the issue lies in counseling and preparing the donor to accept the renunciation of embryos as something good and worthy (Bharadwaj and Glasner 2009).

Hoffmaster (2006 cited in Ballantyne and de Lacey 2008, p. 149) argued that "The stressful circumstances within which the donation of eggs is requested means that they may be susceptible to feelings of obligation and duty that may unduly influence their decision to donate." Women undergoing IVF are dependent upon good relations with their service providers in the hope of a successful outcome of their treatment. The hierarchy between doctors and patients is not conducive to asking questions regarding the fate of their surplus reproductive material. They would not like to jeopardize this relationship and may agree to donate for this reason. In India, the hierarchical relationship is based not only on the classic doctor–patient relationship; rather cultural acceptance of (moral) authority of physicians and other factors such as class, caste, and education gap, which create a power distance, play a role as well (Glasner 2009, Gupta 2010).

Egg donation does not present any prospect of therapeutic benefit for women undergoing IVF. In fact, it threatens the therapeutic process, because women may have to go through repeated cycles of stimulation for egg retrieval if they give away their "surplus" eggs and do not have them fertilized and have the extra embryos cryopreserved. Besides, they run the risk of ovarian hyperstimulation syndrome (including an increased risk of ovarian cancer) and compromised future fertility and its psychological consequences. These risks are often played down, as was the case with the researchers of the report (IOM-NRC 2007), which amounts to misinforming women.

Also, it is difficult to establish whether women are receiving increased hormonal dosage to optimize the "yield." A study in the *Lancet* (Heijnen *et al.* 2007) offered convincing evidence that the best standard of treatment for IVF should *not* need to involve doses of hormones at the levels routinely used in gathering eggs for research. "Mild" or "natural" treatment strategies were proved in a clinical trial to produce as good pregnancy rates as high-dosage therapies. Yet, IVF specialists in India are doing hyper-stimulation and harvesting a large number of eggs.

Drawing on a research ethics framework approach to egg donation advocated by Hyun (2006) Ballantyne and de Lacey (2008, p. 145) argue:

> The principle of "just participation selection" requires that research subjects be selected from the population that stands to benefit from the research. Based on this principle infertile women should be actively recruited to donate eggs for fertility-related research *only*. It is unethical to exclusively or predominantly recruit infertile women to donate eggs for stem cell research that concerns general medical conditions. It is preferable to recruit women from the general population to donate eggs for such research, and these women should be viewed as healthy volunteers. To avoid exploitation, these donors should receive compensation for both the direct and indirect costs associated with their donation.

Taking into account actual and prospective regulations, egg donors for research have been characterized in at least four different ways: as subjects of research, participants in clinical trials, organ donors, or mere tissue or "raw material" providers. To offer them appropriate protection, a new category of research participants – research donors must be recognized (Magnus and Cho 2005). "With such fundamental epistemological disagreement on the status of egg donors and egg donation, it is hardly surprising that governance is unsatisfactory" (Dickenson and Alkorta Idiakez 2008, p. 132).

Baylis and McLeod (2007) argue that all payment schemes that aim to avoid undue inducement of women risk the global exploitation of economically disadvantaged women. The commodification of ova and embryos and the potential exploitation of women "donors" is a matter of grave concern; so is the risk to their health due to hyperstimulation. What is imperative is not only implementation of regulation but oversight and monitoring of clinical and bioethical standards that will strengthen consent procedures and reduce such risks to women who agree to provide ova/embryos for research. To this end public awareness and engagement through debates on this expanding area of research need to be initiated.

Acknowledgements

The research on ova appropriation for this article was conducted within a research project "Body parts, property and gender," funded by a grant from The Netherlands Foundation for the Advancement of Tropical Research (NWO-WOTRO), project number WB 52-871 during the author's affiliation as post-doctoral researcher at Leiden University Medical Center. Sincere thanks are also due to the pregnant women/couples and other respondents who agreed to speak to me. Finally, I thank the anonymous reviewers and Margaret Sleeboom-Faulkner for their very useful comments and suggestions, which helped to improve the manuscript.

References

Ballantyne, A. and de Lacey, S., 2008. Wanted – egg donors for research: a research ethics approach to donor recruitment and compensation. *International Journal of Feminist Approaches to Bioethics*, 1 (2), 145–164.

Baylis, F. and McLeod, C., 2007. The stem cell debate continues: the buying and selling of eggs for research. *Journal of Medical Ethics*, 33 (12), 726–731.

Bharadwaj, A. and Glasner, P., 2009. *Local cells, global science: the rise of embryonic stem cell research in India*. London: Routledge.

Cook, M., 2010. UK fertility watchdog considers sperm and egg market. *BioEdge Newsletter*, 28 August.

DBT-ICMR (Department of Biotechnology and Indian Council for Medical Research), 2007. *Guidelines for stem cell research and therapy*. New Delhi: Indian Council of Medical Research.

Dickenson, D., 2006. The lady vanishes: what's missing from the stem cell debate. *Bioethical Inquiry*, 3, 43–54.

Dickenson, D., 2007. *Property in the body: feminist perspectives*. Cambridge: Cambridge University Press.

Dickenson, D. and Alkorta Idiakez, I., 2008. Ova donation for stem cell research: an international perspective. *International Journal of Feminist Approaches to Bioethics*, 1 (2), 125–144.

Dizikes, P., 2007. Reluctance of egg donors stymies Harvard efforts. *Boston Globe*, 7 June [online]. Available from: http://www.boston.com/yourlife/health/diseases/articles/2007/06/07 [Accessed 24 June 2007].

Frew, S.E., *et al.*, 2007. India's health biotech sector at a crossroads. *Nature Biotechnology*, 25 (4), 403–417.

Glasner, P., 2009. Cellular division: social and political complexity in Indian stem cell research. *New Genetics and Society*, 28 (3), 283–296.

Gupta, J.A., 2010. Exploring Indian women's reproductive decision-making regarding prenatal testing. *Culture, Health and Sexuality*, 12 (2), 191–204.

Gupta, J.A. and Richters, A., 2008. Embodied subjects and fragmented objects: women's bodies, assisted reproduction technologies and the right to self-determination. *Bioethical Inquiry*, 5 (4), 239–249.

Haimes, E. and Taylor, K., 2009. Fresh embryo donation for human embryonic stem cell (hESC) research: the experiences and values of IVF couples asked to be embryo donors. *Human Reproduction*, 24 (9), 2142–2150.

Heijnen, E., *et al.*, 2007. A mild treatment strategy for in-vitro fertilisation: a randomised non-inferiority trial. *Lancet*, 369, 743–749.

HFEA, 2007. Statement on donating eggs for research. Available from: http://www.hfea.gov.uk/en/1491.html [Accessed 22 May 2007].

Hyun, I., 2006. Fair payment or undue inducement. *Nature*, 442 (7103), 629–630.

IOM-NRC (Institute of Medicine and National Research Council), 2007. *Assessing the medical risks of human oocyte donation for stem cell research: workshop report*. Washington, DC: The National Academies Press.

ISSCR (International Society for Stem Cell Research), 2007. *Guidelines for the conduct of human embryonic stem cell research* [online]. Available from: http://www.isscr.org/guidelines/index.htm [Accessed 19 August 2008].

Kim, L., 2008. Explaining the Hwang scandal: national scientific culture and its global relevance. *Science as Culture*, 17 (4), 397–415.

Magnus, D. and Cho, M.K., 2005. Issues in oocyte donation for stem cell research. *Science*, 308, 1747–1748.

Mudur, G.S., 2005. Big wonder cells mess. *The Telegraph*, 20 November.

Resnick, D., 2001. Regulating the market for human eggs. *Bioethics*, 15 (1), 1–25.

Roberts, E., 2007. Extra embryos: the ethics of cryopreservation in Ecuador and elsewhere. *American Ethnologist*, 34 (1), 181–199.

Salter, B., *et al.*, 2006. Stem cells in India: emerging economics and the politics of globalization. Working Paper No. 16, Global Politics Research Group, Norwich.

Scully, J.L. and Rehmann-Sutter, C., 2006. Creating donors: the 2005 Swiss law on donation of "spare" embryos to hESC research. *Bioethical Inquiry*, 3, 81–93.

Sharma, R., 2010. Young Delhi women donating their eggs for quick bucks. *Indo-Asian News Service*, 11 February [online]. Available from: http://www.geneticsandsociety.org/article.php?id5071 [Accessed 20 March 2010].

Sunder Rajan, K., 2007. Experimental values, Indian clinical trials and surplus health. *New Left Review*, 45, May–June, 67–88.

Svendsen, M.N. and Koch, L., 2008. Unpacking the "spare embryo": facilitating stem sell research in a moral landscape. *Social Studies of Science*, 38 (1), 93–110.

Thompson, C., 2005. *Making parents: the ontological choreography of reproductive technology*. Cambridge: MIT Press.

UK Stem Cell Initiative, 2005. *Global positions in stem cell research* [online]. Available from: http://www.dh.gov.uk/ab/UKSCI/index.htm [Accessed 19 August 2008].

Waldby, C., 2008. Oocyte markets: women's reproductive work in embryonic stem cell research. *New Genetics and Society*, 27 (1), 19–31.

Waldby, C. and Mitchell, R., 2006. *Tissue economies: blood, organs, and cell lines in late capitalism*. Durham, NC: Duke University Press.

Modalities of value, exchange, solidarity: the social life of stem cells in China

Achim Rosemann

Department of Social Anthropology, University of Sussex, Brighton, UK

The donation of embryos for human embryonic stem cell (hESC) research is commonly framed as an act of solidarity, exemplifying a selfless expression of help from present-day citizens for public health improvements in the future. As I will show at the case of hESC research in the People's Republic of China, however, such discourse conceals the complexities of contemporary stem cell distribution and exchange systems, as well as the concrete forms of value and benefit that the derivation, use and circulation of these tissues has for user communities already in the here and now. While it is clear that the medical, scientific and commercial hopes of hESC research have not yet materialized, I will show that the current regulatory approach of hESC line distribution in China enables the usage of these materials as a resource of power that can be used strategically for the accrual of various forms of influence and value.

Introduction

The technological ability to alter the human embryo, to open up and redirect its biological potential for therapeutic and economic projects, has given rise to significant alterations of the meanings and manifestations commonly associated with classical terms of economic analysis, such as value, labor, exchange and (re)distribution (Franklin and Lock 2003, Waldby and Mitchell 2006). These processes are accompanied, and simultaneously enabled and legitimized, by transformations in cultural expectations, as well as by reconceptualizations of forms of sociality and subjectivity (*cf.* Hogle 2005).

In this article I shall explore these processes through an analysis of donation and exchange systems of human embryos and their biological derivates in the People's Republic of China. Research findings are based on observations and interviews with 15 stem cell researchers and 15 IVF clinicians in three large cities in Southeast and Central China. The research was conducted between December 2007 and March 2008.

I shall argue that under the current regulatory conditions of embryo donation and hESC distribution in China, a fundamental rift exists between ideas of therapeutic value as they are raised among embryo donors in the context of IVF, and the actual forms of value that are generated by the use of donated embryonic tissues. As I shall exemplify, this is the case not only in present-day systems of hESC exchange and distribution, but is highly likely also in future modalities of therapeutic application. This problem, I argue, is not restricted to China alone, but is endemic to virtually all countries in which scientific, medical and financial achievements of hESC research are likely either to serve only a comparably small segment of the national population, or to create benefits far from their original regional context of production.

The value in and of stem cells

The donation of embryos for hESC research is usually based on a logic of dispossession, which is grounded in a rationality of solidarity and benefit sharing (*cf.* Hayden 2003). The embryo is exchanged for the prospect of future improvements of public health, an outcome that – potentially at least – might benefit others as well as the embryo donor itself. This promissory invocation of healthier futures, as has been widely reported, is closely related to the hope of the generation of economic profits, which has set free considerable flows of capital into speculative therapeutic ventures (*cf.* Helmreich 2008).

Hope thus has emerged as a central element in the discursive, regulatory and performative choreographies through which hESC research is legitimized, governed and financed, and biological materials are procured and distributed (*cf.* Rubin 2008). Brown (2005) has suggested in this context that the reliance of emerging therapeutic markets on expectations of promissory future value signifies a shift from "regimes of truth," in which behavior is structured and resources are mobilized on the basis of established evidence, to "regimes of hope," in which speculative and imaginative invocations of future benefits are elevated to a source of authority and to a guiding principle for economic and scientific action.

Harvey (2009, p. 54), in a related argument, suggests in this context that human embryonic stem cells, if conceived in terms of their bare materiality, have hardly any value, and that it is exclusively their inestimable potential value that elevates them to objects of intensive hope, regulation and investment. Franklin (2007, p. 53), on the other hand, in her discussion of stem cells as a form of "livestock," provides a more encompassing discussion of the value of hESCs, which addresses also their present-day value. Similar to the ways in which sheep formed the "stud stock capital of the world" in the nineteenth century, the careful husbandry and banking of stem cells today form an important source of research and capital value that constitutes the indispensable basis for contemporary bioresearch industries to function. But also for Franklin, the full realization of the capital value of the currently existing stock of stem cells depends largely on the successful translation of the inherent biological potentialities of these cells into projects of life and health enhancement; a process whose outcomes are still to be proven.

In this article, I propose to abandon, at least temporarily, an analytical perspective that focuses on the promissory and future aspects of hESC research. Instead, in this article, it is the immediate and tangible value of human embryonic stem cells I am interested in: their capacity as research materials endowed with direct forms of use value and emotions, exchanged among laboratories and used by skilled hands in interlinked chains of culturing and experimentation. More concretely, by looking into the specificities of this particular material domain, and into the precise ways in which these cellular materials are employed in daily laboratory routines, I shall illustrate how hESCs become the basic substance for the creation of emerging cultural practices, and for the actualization of new forms of value (*cf.* Miller 2002). First, however, I shall draw the attention to the ways in which the value of embryos is communicated to donors in the context of IVF.

Forecasting hope to donors: healthier futures and the solidaric self

The crucial role played by women to bring the embryos used in hESC research into being is often neglected in debates on the value of hESCs. In contrast to the contribution of sperm, the induced maturation and removal of oocytes in the IVF clinic is a physically risky and emotionally demanding process that involves long-drawn-out regimes of medical examination and drug administration, which end up in a dicey surgical procedure. In fact, it is this arduous process of "women's reproductive labor" (Dickenson 2006, p. 43) that forms the vital core of a new and rapidly increasing research economy and which lies at the center of all present-day and future benefits (*cf.* Waldby and Cooper 2006, Svendsen and Koch 2008).

A crucial question that arises here is: what ideas are projected into the minds of embryo donors, so that the donation of their spare embryos appears not only justifiable, but reasonable, or even desirable? While there is no space here to discuss these points in detail, and a more inclusive analysis can be found elsewhere (Rosemann 2009), I shall highlight here some central characteristics that seem exemplary for the situation in China as a whole.

A quasi-universal core claim of hESC research is, of course, that the embryos provided are used for the finding of cures for severe and today still incurable diseases. In the context of China, at least in the institutes I visited, these projected scenarios of healthier futures were usually defined in terms of a clearly demarcated national citizenry and territory. As one of the doctors with whom I spoke put it: "We tell our patients that *the whole society* may benefit from the donation of their embryos in the future" (emphasis mine). Embryo donation, thus, is framed here clearly as an act of altruism and solidarity, a selfless expression of help from present-day citizens for improving the health of fellow citizens in the future.

As I intend to show in the following sections of this article, these representations of the future value of donated embryos, in terms of their contributions to an imagined national community, offer both a one-sided but also distorted picture of the real and potentially real benefits and beneficiaries of hESC research in China. Three points of contemplation deserve attention here.

Complexifications

First, the scattering of places in which research is carried out implies also the spatial dispersion of therapeutic applications. As I shall show, the distribution of stem cell lines across borders is about to result in the extraction of benefits that are shared beyond the relations of national citizenship, events that are considerably at odds with the expectations that have been raised among embryo donors, who are made to believe that research findings contribute in the first place to the public health of the national community. A well-grounded concern here is that access to these developing therapeutic possibilities will be highly selective, not only across national borders but also within. Unlike the donation of blood, for example, which benefits people regardless of their socio-economic status, the donation of embryos for labor-, technology- and capital-intensive hESC research is likely to benefit more wealthy population segments only. While it is true that the development of stem cell based therapies is foreseen to reduce healthcare related costs in the future, in low income countries with highly selective access to high quality healthcare, such as China or India, larger parts of the populations may attain access to these stem cell therapies only under severe constraints and sacrifice. This may include the majority of people who had once donated their embryos for research (Cooper 2008).

Second, the one-sided focus on the communication of the health value of stem cell research neglects in fact all other forms of potential value that are likely to be extracted on the basis of hESC research in the future, among which are: (a) the accrual of financial profits on the part of biotech or pharmaceutical companies; (b) the realization of political ambitions and projects; and (c) the career prospects and financial gains of individual scientists and research institutes.

Third, the narrow focus on the communication of the future therapeutic value of hESC research neglects completely to account for the concrete forms of value and benefit that the derivation, use, distribution and circulation of hESC lines generates among scientific user communities in the present. These tangible, but from the public eye largely hidden, forms of value, as I shall illustrate, range from expanding workforce to an augmented number of publications, to the initiation of national and international research collaborations that bear the potential to result in sustained and mutually beneficial chains of exchanges. These matters have remained entirely unspecified not only in the everyday practice of embryo donation, but also in the academic literature.

Embryonic value and the role of state regulation

To better understand how scientists succeed in transforming hESCs into a tool through which resources and particular forms of value and influence are mobilized at present, it is first necessary to gain insights into the concrete regulatory conditions under which the transfer and exchange of established stem cell lines are carried out (*cf.* Sleeboom-Faulkner and Patra 2008). Compared to the UK, where the distribution of hESC lines is organized entirely through the centralized control of the UK Stem Cell Bank (UK-SCB), the movement of hESC lines in China occurs in a more open and, in a regulatory sense, also a less stringent system.[1] But let us first look at the situation in the UK. In the UK the transfer of hESC lines is permitted only after the completion of a wide range of meticulously prescribed check-up procedures, which range from informed consent protocols to standardized assessment procedures for cell characterization and quality control. The UK-SCB steering committee plays a crucial role here, as it checks the license, qualifications, reputation, research objectives and capacities of applicant centers. In case of requests from centers abroad, the committee still evaluates the legality of the proposed research project in the acquiring country (Stephens *et al.* 2008, p. 49). A further responsibility of the committee is to negotiate with applicant centers the precise conditions and terms of use of the attained cell materials. Agreed conditions must fully comply with the UK-SCB's code of practice. Transgression is punishable in law (Warrell *et al.* 2009).

This situation differs significantly from China, where individual research institutes manage the distribution of hESC samples, and regional government branches carry out the necessary controls. Furthermore, a huge difference exists in China regarding the transfer of hESC materials within and across national borders. While transfers of hESC samples within China seem to occur on the basis of the institutes' internal approval procedures, a considerably more complex regulatory picture emerges in the case of transfers of hESC samples abroad.[2] Here, two basic requirements must be met. The first is to obtain approval from the Chinese Inspection and Quarantine Bureau, which handles an online registration system, and which has specified the conditions that apply to the transfer of human tissue in the "Work Norms for the Health Quarantine Examination and Approval of the Entry/Exit of Special (Biological) Items," a nationally binding memorandum issued in 2006.[3] No distinct set of specifications, however, exists for the transfer of hESC samples in this document, which fall under the same category as blood, bone marrow, cord blood and other tissue commonly used for medical purposes. Documentation requirements for this category include a range of standard operation procedures for the identification of cell identity, quality and the presence of microbial contaminants and biohazards. Further requirements include a description of research purposes and potential risks.

The second requirement is the setting up of a Material Transfer Agreement (MTA), a document that has to be signed by the Chinese Human Genetic Resources Control Office (HGCO). The MTA specifies the conditions and terms of use of exchanged tissue as negotiated and agreed upon between the exchange partners. Besides issues related to intellectual property and benefit sharing, the document must include a technical description of the research, and a risk assessment and safety evaluation form. The HGCO checks also the license and qualifications of the tissue recipient abroad. Once the MTA has been authorized, a local branch of the Inspection and Quarantine Bureau issues a final approval document (Warrell *et al.* 2009).

A key difference from the UK is that neither the HGCO nor the Inspection and Quarantine Bureau carry out controls of issues relevant to the ethical oversight of the transfer of hESC samples, such as the documentation of appropriate informed consent. Furthermore, while research purposes and related risks, together with the license, reputation and capacities of tissue recipients are assessed in case of international transfers, in domestic transfers such controls are performed by individual research institutes. As shall be shown in the next section, these differences have wide-ranging consequences.

Stem cell distribution in China

A key purpose of the UK-SCB is to operate as a "neutral intermediary," which fulfills important functions of ethical oversight, but simultaneously maximizes open and fast access to cell lines for qualified researchers (Glasner 2005, p. 357). As my data indicate, such a model of open access to hESC lines as established in the UK is far from being attained in China, where only a relatively small number of institutes can establish these lines, of which even fewer are willing to share their resources unreservedly with others. Not surprisingly then, it was a frequently heard complaint among Chinese researchers that it was extremely difficult to obtain hESC lines in China – a fact that might explain why a larger number of researchers rely primarily on stem cell lines imported from the US. Hence, compared to the centrally regulated distribution system of hESC lines in the UK, the institute-centered distribution approach in China clearly privileges those nstitutes that can establish stem cell lines themselves, but it creates dependency structures and disadvantages for those who have to rely on the supply by others.

As I shall show in the following sections, as a result of the scarcity of fully characterized hESC lines and of the absence of a regulatory approach that allows open access to these materials, hESC samples are turned into a strategic resource of power that can be used in well-calculated ways for the accrual of various forms of value and influence. These hidden and in the literature largely unexplored forms of value extraction of hESC exchange systems can be accounted for in the regulatory environment of China at least in four different ways.

Strategic games of inclusion and exclusion

If a research institute or hospital department that intends to carry out hESC research does not preside over the technical, biological or financial resources to derive hESC lines itself, it is entirely dependent on the supply of cell materials by others. Research centers that have created hESC lines, in turn, decide very carefully to whom and for which purposes they provide their lines. As was mentioned by researchers in several of the institutions I visited, requests to obtain or distribute lines were frequently rejected. While one reason behind this reluctance arises from the fear that distributed hESC lines might be used in irresponsible or unqualified ways, another cause is constituted by concerns about the rise of potential competitors. A senior researcher in one of the centers I visited put it as follows:

> In this field there is strong competition. Everyone wants to get more results and publish papers faster than others. Some centers think, if they give you a line, this might endanger their own position, so … they just don't want to give it to you.

Researchers in China are not alone in experiencing such kinds of fears. Similar assumptions underlie, for example, the conclusions of research by McCormick *et al.* (2007) on hESC line distribution systems in the US, who wonder whether the widespread and global distribution of hESC samples from US labs (especially from the universities of Wisconsin and Harvard) do not provide researchers elsewhere with the resources that in the final instance might harm the domestic research environment in the US (2007, p. 1).

In China's research community, however, such ideas on the strategic withholding of stem cell materials (but expressed in a scenario not of international, but interinstitutional competition) are not shared unanimously. At least three of the scientists I spoke to strongly opposed such forms of calculated inclusion or exclusion, arguing that such practices would prevent scientific progress rather than promote it. As one of these researchers put it, the only criteria that should apply in deciding on the request of another center are the institute's financial situation, its technical abilities and scientific credibility.

However, in a regulatory environment in which open access to hESC materials is not institutionally anchored, the opportunities of exploiting the assumed benefits of a particularistic mode of hESC distribution may, for some researchers at least, simply be too tempting. Accordingly, strategies of calculated withholding or, as shall be explored in the next sections, the tactical delivery of cell materials to mobilize resources and initiate research collaborations, seems, at least in the centers I visited, a common pattern rather than an exception.

Influencing research agendas, harvesting labor

The scarcity of fully characterized hESC lines in a context of high demand elevates these tissues to a central element in the creation of research alliances, collaborations and networks. Sometimes, centers that possess sufficient cell materials to distribute samples to other institutes can strategically use these exchanges to advance their own research interests. This is true in particular in the case of more renowned centers that, in addition to their command over biological resources, also possess the technologies, skills, knowledge and experience required to work with the hESC lines they distribute. In collaborations with local partners these features may function as important resources of control. As was mentioned by the director of one of the larger institutes I visited:

> We distribute lines to several universities, they collaborate with us and then we need to transfer techniques, we need to transfer cell lines, and we also control the different phases of the research. But if we send our lines out of our city, to Beijing for example, they have their own ideas; they just do it by themselves. We just collaborate in [the sense of] – if you publish, then you mention that the cell lines are from us.

Possession of and command over hESC lines, in combination with the knowledge, skills and technology of how to conduct state of the art research, thus seem to provide these centers with a certain degree of authority. Dependency structures that result from the limited access to hESC lines are used to indirectly determine and profit from the research and manpower of collaborating partner institutes – at least, if these are located in the same geographic area.

In the case of the above-mentioned center, for example, influence is exerted through the selection of associates whose research interests correlate positively with their own research agenda, as well as through regular meetings and seminars with collaborating partners, which are used for processes of feedback, coaching and the provision of additional training, in addition to the presentation and sharing of research findings. Another way in which the institute that provides hESC lines to collaborating partners generates value is by laboratory training of research students from affiliated or partner institutes. To understand this point better, it is important to know that the laboratory training of postgraduate students in China lasts up to two full years (at Master's level, which lasts three years altogether). In this period, it is a common practice for students, besides their coursework and own experiments, to carry out large quantities of work for the research of senior staff in the host institute. As several young career researchers told me, only in year three of their Master's training did they get more freedom and were able to concentrate on their own research more extensively.

HESC lines as building blocks of international collaborations

A third way in which the inherent capacities of hESC lines are translated into benefits and value for the research centers that possess and distribute these materials, is by using these lines as initial gifts in the initiation of research collaborations with research institutes abroad, especially with prestigious centers in the US, Europe, or Japan. Collaborations with international partners not only raise the status of a particular center, but they bring with them a wide range of opportunities, such as an increased likelihood of attracting funding, better opportunities for high profile publications and improved chances for the discovery of significantly outstanding findings.

An example in China is a recently established research collaboration between a center in China and a center in the US. The pivotal point of this partnership is formed by the distribution of a disease-specific hESC line, which has been derived on the basis of embryos from persons who are carriers of a monogenetic disease that is relatively widespread in China. The line, created in the Chinese center, is the first of its kind in the world, and due to the scarcity of embryos with these characteristics its replication is rather difficult. The transfer of the line has enabled the initiation of a larger and long-term research project that for technical and financial reasons could not have been carried out by the center in China alone. The results and benefits of this project are shared equally among the partners: an agreement that, according to the director of the Chinese partner institute, is clearly advantageous for his center.

HESC line transfer as starting point of longer exchange chains

If, as in the previous example, an initial collaborative project between international partners has been successful, it can happen that the partnership is prolonged and extended to additional domains of activity. The transfer of stem cell lines, at least when these actually formed the initial point of that alliance, have then instigated a longer chain of exchanges that comprises persons, goods and services of several kinds. Such international partnerships produce value for a variety of reasons, but key factors here are the exploitation of differences in regulatory structures as well as the stratification of prices and labor costs across spatial boundaries. As I realized in the instance of another intensive and long-term China–USA research collaboration, the USA partner profited from the alliance in at least two ways: the carrying out of experiments in a low cost environment, and the exploitation of regulatory differences concerning the usage of research animals. This advantage is made possible because the Chinese regulations on animal use offer more freedom than those in the US.

The benefits from this intercontinental hESC collaboration flow, at least in this case, evenly in both directions. Forms of value generated by the Chinese laboratory include a general improvement of status, the exchange of researchers, the receiving of biological materials, lab equipment, technologies, information, and a significant increase in joint publications in high impact journals. Furthermore, joint applications for funding in China have strongly increased the financial basis of the center, which now has succeeded in fostering its position in a regional and national, as well as international, context.

While it is important to realize that in this case the exchange of hESC lines was preceded by a strong interpersonal bond between the heads of these two centers, it is also clear that here the distribution of hESC lines has constituted an initial and central action on which basis further exchanges and collaborative practices were built. In this case, however, the initial gift was provided from the center in the US: a sample of a hESC line derived by James Thompson, which was used for the characterization of at least six newly derived lines in China, which are now used in experiments across both sides of the Pacific Ocean.

Conclusions

In this article I have shown that under the specific regulatory conditions through which the distribution of human embryonic stem cells is carried out in China, these materials are turned into a resource of influence and value that can be used strategically for the extraction of various forms of symbolic, social, scientific and capital value, that include the influencing of research agendas, the receiving of additional manpower, increased numbers of publications, the opening of possibilities for international collaborations as well as extended exchange chains among long-term partners that comprise technology, knowledge, access to research animals and the like.

The integration of hESC lines into new relational networks and systems of exchange does not mean, of course, their integration into a purchase economy, in which the use value of these tissues is transformed into monetary forms of exchange value, and traded on a market. Instead, the exchanges referred to display characteristics typical of informal patronage systems on the one hand, and reciprocal gift economies on the other. Boundaries between gift and commodity economies in these described exchange patterns, however, were highly blurred (*cf.* Waldby and Mitchell 2006). By forming the initial step in longer chains of exchanges and interactions, the distribution of hESC lines from one laboratory to another as a gift can be seen to constitute a strategic form of action through which collaborating partners aim to foster the position and functioning of their laboratories in a political research economy that increasingly aims toward the commercialization of scientific findings according to corporate principles. Human embryonic stem cell lines play an interesting part in these processes. In their role as a primary gift, they function as a sort of "exchange token," that is, as a symbolic carrier of value, whose distribution results in the return of goods, information or services at a later point in time.

In the light of these findings, Harvey's assessment (2009, p. 54), referred to above, that human embryonic stem cells, before the successful translation of their biological potential into therapeutic and monetary value, hardly have any value, cannot be maintained in this way. While it is clear that the belief in the promissory future potential of these tissues underlies and animates present-day systems of hESC exchanges, it is equally clear that these materials, in the immediate context of their production and (international) circulation, do simultaneously, acquire and generate forms of value – long before the translation of their inherent biological potentialities into new therapeutic projects and economies is realized.

Taken together, these insights do not only refer to the blank spaces in contemporary informed consent procedures, but they clarify also that further research into the use of stem cells as "open" or "closed" biological sources is needed (*cf.* Hope

2008), in order to understand how institutionally imposed proprietary restrictions shape the present-day realities of the scientific projects that take us into our regenerative futures.

Acknowledgements

The research for this article formed part of the International Science and Bioethics Collaborations Project, an ESRC funded joint research program of the Universities of Cambridge, Durham and Sussex (grant number RES-062-23-0215). I am grateful in particular to Margaret Sleeboom-Faulkner and Marilyn Strathern for their comments, as well as to four anonymous reviewers, who generously offered plenty of highly valuable suggestions and additional insights.

Notes

1. This situation is about to change with the construction of five stem cell banks in China, which shall be taken into service in 2013.
2. Two researchers told me they had distributed various hESC samples to other labs, entirely without any form of official approval. These transfers were solely based on the setting up of a Material Transfer Agreement between the two labs.
3. The document can be found online at http://wsjyjgs.aqsiq.gov.cn/xzxk/rcjtswpwsjysp/200610/ t20061024_2192.htm [Accessed 10 April 2011]. Many thanks at this point to one of the two anonymous reviewers for providing me with this information.

References

Brown, N., 2007. Shifting tenses: reconnecting regimes of truth hope? *Configurations*, 13 (3), 331–355.

Cooper, M., 2008. Experimental labour – offshoring clinical trials to China. *East Asian Science, Technology and Society*, 2 (1), 73–92.

Dickenson, D., 2006. The lady vanishes: what's missing from the stem cell debate. *Biotechnical Inquiry*, 3, 43–54.

Franklin, S., 2007. *Dolly mixtures: the remaking of genealogy*. Durham, NC: Duke University Press.

Franklin, S. and Lock, M., 2003. Animation and cessation: the remaking of life and death. *In*: S. Franklin and M. Lock, eds. *Remaking life and death: toward an anthropology of the biosciences*. Santa Fe: School of American Research Press, 3–23.

Glasner, P., 2005. Banking on immortality? Exploring the stem cell supply chain from embryo to therapeutic application. *Current Sociology*, 53 (2), 355–366.

Harvey, O., 2009. Human embryonic stem cell research in the United States: some policy options for industry development. *Politics & Policy*, 37 (1), 51–71.

Hayden, C., 2003. *When nature goes public: the making and unmaking of bioprospecting in Mexico*. Princeton, NJ: Princeton University Press.

Helmreich, S., 2008. Species of biocapital. *Science as Culture*, 17 (4), 463–478.

Hogle, L.F., 2005. Enhancement technologies and the body. *Annual Review of Anthropology*, 34, 695–715.

Hope, J., 2008. *Biobazaar: the open source revolution and biotechnology*. Cambridge, MA: Harvard University Press.

McCormick, J.B., Scott, C.T., and Owen Smith, J.D., 2007. Distribution of hESC lines: how, when where? [online]. Available from: http://bioethics.stanford.edu/stemcells/documents/ISSCRMTA.pdf [Accessed 19 November 2007].

Miller, D., 2002. *Material cultures: why some things matter*. Chicago: University of Chicago Press.

Rosemann, A., 2009. The IVF-stem cell interface in China: ontologies, value-perceptions and donation-practices of embryonic forms of life. *In*: O. Doering, ed. *Life sciences in translation – a Sino-European dialogue on ethical governance of the life sciences*. BIONET Textbook delivery to the EU Commission, 168–178 [online]. Available from: http://www.lse.ac.uk/BIOS/research/ BIONET [Accessed 10 April 2011].

Rubin, B., 2008. Therapeutic promise in the discourse of human embryonic stem cell research. *Science as Culture*, 17 (1), 13–27.

Sleeboom-Faulkner, M. and Patra, P.K., 2008. The bioethical vacuum: national policies on human embryonic stem cell research in India and China. *Journal of International Bioethics and Law*, 5 (1), 221–234.

Stephens, N., Atkinson, P. and Glasner, P., 2008. The UK stem cell bank: Securing the past, validating the present, protecting the future. *Science as Culture*, 17 (1), 43–56.

Svendsen, M.N. and Koch, L., 2008. Unpacking the "spare embryo": facilitating stem cell research in a moral landscape. *Social Studies of Science*, 38 (1), 93–110.

Waldby, C. and Cooper, M.,2006. The biopolitics of reproduction: post Fordist biotechnology and women's clinical labor. Working Paper No.15, Global Biopolitics Research Group, King's College London [online]. Available from: http://www.kcl.ac.uk/content/1/c6/03/03/65/wp15. pdf [Accessed 10 April 2011].

Waldby, C. and Mitchell, R., 2006. *Tissue economies: blood, organs, and cell lines in late capitalism*. Durham, NC: Duke University Press.

Warrell, D. et al., 2009. Cure Committee Report: China–UK Research Ethics. UK Medical Research Council [online]. http://www.mrc.ac.uk/Utillities/Documentrecord/index.htm?d=MRC006303 [Accessed 20 April 2011].

Scientific institutions and effective governance: a case study of Chinese stem cell research

Joy Yueyue Zhang

BIOS Centre, Sociology Department, London School of Economics and Political Science, London, UK

In terms of stem cell research, China appears both as a "powerhouse" armed with state-of-the-art facilities, internationally trained personnel and permissive regulation and as a "bit player," with its capability for conducting high quality research still in question. The gap between China's assiduous endeavors and the observed outcome is due to a number of factors. Based on interviews with 48 key stakeholders active in Chinese stem cell research, this article examines how the structure of scientific institutions has affected effective governance in China. It is demonstrated that despite China's recent efforts to attract highly competent researchers and to launch new regulatory initiatives, the effects of these attempts have been diminished by an absence of middle-layer positions within research teams and by the uncoordinated administrative structures among regulatory bodies.

Introduction

Existing data on China's life science development often depicts two different stories, both of which are true: on the one hand, China has been most assiduous in promoting scientific advancement. During the period of 1995 to 2005, China's R&D expenditure sustained an annual average growth rate of more than 18% (OECD 2007a). Yet on the other hand, in terms of China's patent and publication per unit of investment, the "growth rate of scientific productivity of China's S&T institutes has been negative since the 1990s" (Huang, Varum and Gouveia 2006, p. 453). In addition, in recent decades, the Chinese government has been most active in rewarding and improving professional excellence, which has attracted an increasing number of scientific personnel trained abroad to join its scientific force (Fox 2007, Schaaper 2009). However, the old rule of "an inclination toward competition and secrecy, rather than openness" (Solo and Pressberg 2007, p. 106) is still predominant among Chinese researchers (Hao and Liu 2005). As one of the expanding fields in China, the development of stem cell research also hosts two conflicting images

(DTI 2004, UK Stem Cell Initiative (UKSCI) 2005). To paraphrase Murray and Spar's (2006) findings, in terms of stem cell research, China appears both as a "powerhouse" armed with state-of-the-art facilities, internationally trained personnel and permissive regulation and as a "bit player" with its capability for conducting high quality research still in question.

As with all national governance strategies, there are a number of factors worth investigating to comprehend the gap between China's endeavors and the observed outcomes. Effective governance theorist, Morten Egeberg has pointed out that discussions on regulatory effectiveness often concentrate on seeking behavioral, cultural or procedural explanations, while showing a lack of interest in how organizational structures "might intervene in policy processes and ultimately shape policy outputs" (Egeberg 1999, p. 155, Egeberg 2003). This is to say, institutional arrangements may affect "actual decision behaviour," as well as influence "coordination, choices and implementation" (Egeberg 2003, p. 116). Current research on China's stem cell governance seems to exhibit a situation similar to what Egeberg described. Existing literature has offered many rich descriptions of particular aspects of Chinese stem cell governance, such as clinical application (Chen 2009), problem framing in basic research (Sleeboom-Faulkner and Patra 2008), economic incentives (Salter *et al.* 2006) and governance participation (Salter and Qiu 2009, Zhang 2010a). Yet how existing institutional *structures* affect the translation of governance initiatives into practice seems to have been less explored. This article provides an initial empirical discussion on China's institutional arrangement and its relation to effective governance in stem cell research. It expands upon arguments made by the author in previously published work (Zhang 2010b). The focus is not to assess individual R&D policy *per se*, but to investigate how existing structures at the micro- and macro-levels (i.e. research group and ministerial level) shape actual policy outcomes.

Data used in this article forms part of a larger study on China's stem cell governance funded by the Wellcome Trust. In 2008, a total of 48 semi-structured interviews were conducted in six cities (Beijing, Tianjin, Changsha, Shanghai, Hangzhou and Guangzhou). Interviewees consist of two Ministry of Health officials, one former popular science editor, seven bioethicists, and 38 stem cell researchers. Each interview was recorded, transcribed and sorted into themes according to reoccurring concepts (Corbin and Strauss 1990). This article contributes to the ongoing discussion on the observed gap between Chinese stakeholders' input and expected research output. It indicates that one of the possible factors impeding effective governance in China's bioscience is the lack of institutional structural adaptations.

Scientific institutions and their role in innovation governance

Before investigating structural influence on the implementation of R&D policies, it is necessary to first clarify why the "institutional milieu" (Morgan 1997, p. 493) is considered to be important to innovation. Previous studies have highlighted two aspects (Rey-Rocha *et al.* 2002, Reagans and McEvily 2003 and Burau *et al.* 2009). First, structural configurations constitute the context in which information flow and decision-making take place within and between existing organizations, such as research institutions and regulatory agencies. Secondly, institutional structures embody and promote norms, routines, and social conventions, which provide the setting that constrains or enables innovative agents' research goals and interests. Innovation system scholar Joseph Leibovitz more explicitly highlighted the function of institutions in facilitating collective learning and nurturing inter-organizational collaborations. He argues that institutions have a key *"co-ordinative role* in terms of reinforcing norms, routines, trust and collaboration within the process of innovation" (Leibovitz 2003, p. 2615, original emphasis). When such roles are not fulfilled, the institution may post barriers to regulatory efficiency. Furthermore, research on national regulatory contexts and biomedical research capacity building have also indicated that besides individual skills development and organizational practices, structural features of research teams and "supra-organizational" support are also vital to R&D efficiency (Cooke 2005, pp. 46–47; see also Albert and Mickan 2003, DOH 2004).

Following this line of enquiry, this article investigates how at both the micro- and macro-levels, China's institutional structures for stem cell research accommodate various research directives. The first section examines micro-level structures, namely the building of research teams. Data suggests that, in many cases, there is a common deficiency in research positions between the team's top level (the professor) and the broad bottom level (research students). In spite of China's recent administrative incentives in attracting global scientific talent, research efficiency may be hampered by the absence of "middle-layer researchers," who serve as the key for team-level exchange of ideas and coordination. In the second section, this article investigates macro-level structure and its connection to effective policy implementation. It is demonstrated that China's recent scientific governance strategies might have been overshadowed by uncoordinated jurisdiction arrangements among different national institutions, such as the Ministry of Health (MOH) and the Ministry of Science and Technology (MOST).

Team structures and micro-level inefficiency

Governing initiatives: single spark set the prairie afire?

At the 2007 National Award Conference for Science and Technology, China's Premier Wen Jiabao highlighted that "the real fuel for scientific progress is research personnel. The greater number of excellent research personnel one country has the more advantage for that country to become the leader in science and technology" (Wen, 2007). The ethos of promoting individual excellence as the core of scientific governance has been reflected in a series of Chinese funding incentives launched since the early 1990s.[1] This is further backed by the State Council (China's highest executive branch) issuance of the State's Decision on Further Strengthening Personnel Development Programs (State Council China 2004 2003) and MOST's recent funding schemes' amendments in attracting more overseas-return scientists (MOST 2007). As the Chinese saying goes "a single spark can set the prairie afire." In the case of the life sciences, key researchers with the appropriate knowledge/experience are seen as the "sparks" or the main force to push China's development forward.

The emphasis the Chinese government lays on professional distinction has successfully created enthusiasm among researchers in obtaining rigorous professional training and better communication skills with overseas partners. Overseas-returns are now the backbone in bringing international experience and fresh ideas into China (He 2008, Schaaper 2009). Half of the 38 researchers I interviewed in China have various types of training experience abroad. The ratio of international experience is even higher among those in senior positions. Among the 21 senior scientists interviewed, 14 have acquired doctoral or post-doc training in Western institutions.

Flat team structure

Despite hundreds of researchers returning to China every year with the expectation of being the "sparks" to initiate regional scientific advancement, the "prairie" of the life sciences has not yet been ignited as anticipated. In fact, China's publications in internationally recognized journals are still low both in terms of quantity and quality (Wang and Wang 2006, Corbyn 2008). Moreover, during my fieldwork, interviewees expressed a shared anxiety that most researchers who have demonstrated high proficiency abroad find it difficult to keep up with their research productivity once settled back in China. One recurring reason indicated by Chinese scientists is that in contrast to the considerable development in scientific practice and supportive policies, the institutional structure of scientific teams has shown little change in the past decade. One Chinese senior scientist, currently based at King's College London, described the circumstances of Chinese researchers as isolated islands.

Scientist 01: I have a very good friend who used to work at NIH, returned to China a few years ago . . . I am worried that he cannot maintain the level of research as he used to at NIH. He can't, although he was generously given lots of funds. The government invested 100 million RMB to establish a lab in Peking University . . . Lots of money, but he is not able to keep up with his research.

Interviewer: Is it because of lack of research personnel or of management issues?

Scientist 01: Personnel! Just think about it, he returned with no other people in his lab, and his new employees are all PhD students. Research project cannot be accomplished in this way. The biggest problem China facing now is that the only inferior to a professor is PhD student, there is no way to build a "team."

Interviewer: Why is it hard to build a team in China?

Scientist 01: Too many professors. It's not like in the West, where a professor for example, me, I have three lectures, then senior post-docs, then several post-docs, then some PhD students. It's a team where everybody has different roles, makes different contributions ... In China, everybody is a professor; everybody works on their own project; there is no connection between groups. Everybody is their own team-leader. Thus it's hard to make progress.

As pointed out by this respondent, in terms of scientific productivity, it is not just the *professional qualification* of research personnel that matters, but also the *structural arrangement* of these talents. Greater within-team heterogeneity (meaning diverse tasks held by team members) and synergies among members' expertise are positively related with research efficiency (Magjuka and Baldwin 1991, Katzenbach and Smith 1993). Scientist 01's own team in London is one such example, in which the majority of research personnel take up various positions between the team leader and the broad bottom layer, the students. In the Chinese context, however, Scientist 01 pointed out the problem lies in a thin "middle layer" in the team structure. This is to say apart from the "professor" (Scientist 01's friend), the other members of the team were "all PhD students." Despite the generous funding, administrative support and highly capable principal investigators (PIs), the Chinese situation that concerned this respondent was that "there is no way to build a 'team.'"

This insufficiency in middle-layer positions appeared to be not unusual in Chinese science. In fact, among the 22 Chinese research teams I visited in early 2008, six have the bare structure of "one professor and many students."[2] Even in cases where positions such as associate professors and research fellows do exist, they are more nominal positions than actual functioning members within a team. One such example is from the key laboratory in Nankai University.

I have two associate professors in my team and one technician with undergraduate training ... I did a count the other day, in this academic year we have about 30 students [in my lab], undergraduates, masters, PhDs ... My two assistants [the two associate professors] don't participate in laboratory works ... Well, they are my assistants. I could give them assignments, ask them to contribute to the research, but they are relatively independent ... In comparison [with PIs in Western teams], I have less commanding authority over them. (Scientist 06)

Scientist 06 echoed Scientist 01's comparison between the more complex, multi-layer, fully competent team in the West and the rather flat team structure in China, where "the only inferior to a professor is PhD student." Scientist 06's team constitutes 34 members, with one professor (the respondent), two associate professors, one technician and 30 students. The staff–student ratio already seems alarmingly low. Yet in reality, the situation is worse. As put forward by Scientist 06, the two middle-layer researchers are rather nominal members of the team who are "relatively independent." By drawing on Chinese researchers' accounts, the key structural difference between "inefficient" (reported by

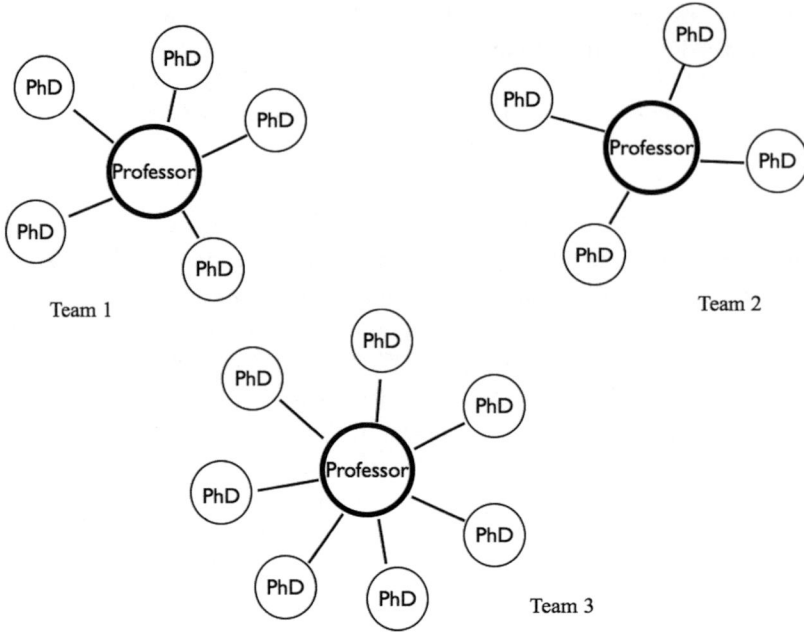

Figure 1. Inefficient teams structure in the eyes of interviewees.

interviewees as common in the Chinese context) and "efficient" (associated by interviewees with "Western") teams can be demonstrated by the graphs in Figures 1 and 2.

In summary, according to interviewees, a productive team structure constitutes researchers with diverse professional ranks, who take up different branches of the research and cooperate at different levels. Yet many respondents identified a popular model of Chinese teams as isolated research islands, in which skilled researchers are separated into many independent one-professor-many-students research groups.

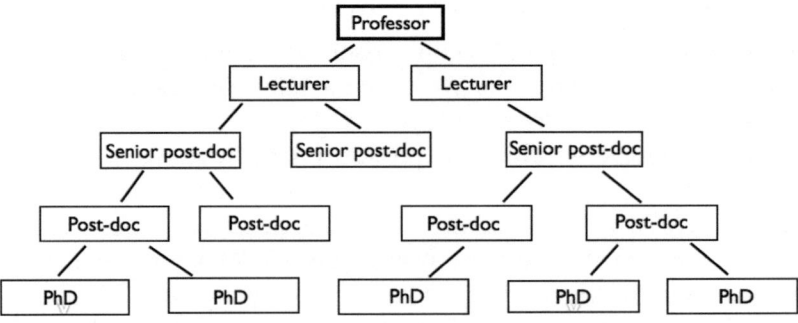

Figure 2. Efficient team structure in the eyes of interviewees.

Intra-team support and inter-team communication

As little attention has been paid to teams' *structural* reforms, the output from China's investment in overseas-return scientific talents seemed to be impeded by the missing middle layer in research groups. Two consequences of this structural barrier to effective governance are most visible: (a) the flat team structure led to teams' internal inefficiency in the comprehension and application of knowledge, or the inadequacy of intra-team support; and (b) structural inadequacy in accommodating middle-layer researchers diverted personnel to establishing their own independent research units. In some cases, this has created unnecessary social barriers for research collaborations. This section analyzes these two consequences in turn.

First, the recurring term in Chinese scientists' explanation of internal inefficiency is the absence of "stage," as one scientist in Peking University Stem Cell Research Centre put it:

> My impression is that in Western research institutions, once you got a new idea, [supposing that financial and legal conditions allow] you can almost immediately start laboratory works to test your hypothesis, because there are other experienced researchers in the group who together could provide you with a stable stage to carry out your plan. But in China, there is no such stage in the group. However great your idea is, you have to start from scratch, say from culturing cell line or other basic laboratory works (Scientist 14).

Scientist 14 pointed out that contemporary research relies as much on the novelty of ideas as on a "stable stage" in which these innovative ideas can be appropriately tested. This professional "stage" within the team requires diverse expertise which a bare "professor–student" structure cannot offer. In other words, R&D objectives cannot be sustained solely on one person's (the professor's) distinction, but also require a structural arrangement (a "stage") which can host a combination of professional expertise. Another respondent in the Chinese Academy of Sciences further explained team structure and its effects on knowledge transfer efficiency:

> I don't think it's fair to say that overseas-returns' individual research efficiency decreases when they settle back in China. They are the same person. But they no longer have the stage to facilitate their work. The output of a research lab has a lot to do with its "intellectual deposits" … In my view, both the accumulation, or say the deposit of knowledge/data and the deposit of research personnel are important in producing quality papers … say if a group has been doing stem cell research for 10 years, of course this group has a bigger research advantage, for it has set up a stage … But if all you have are new comers, or new teams, you need a long time before [the research] finally gets on track. (Scientist 31)

It is again highlighted that individual team productivity depends on the accumulated efforts from experienced professionals, or what Scientist 31 noted as "intellectual deposits." In the eyes of interviewees, a team that can stably host skilled researchers in the middle layer, which forms the scaffold of team support, has a "bigger research advantage" in facilitating the realization of members' scientific potential. In contrast, if a group mainly relies on inexperienced "new comers," with the convention of junior scientists aiming at setting up their "new teams" immediately after acquiring some experience, then the chance to develop a strong intra-team platform is slim. It may even take "a long time before [the research] finally gets on track," not to mention yields results.

Furthermore, as many of the potential middle-layer researchers head their own team instead, the increase in the number of solitary research units also implies growing social boundaries in the field of stem cell research, which in effect increased the difficulty for inter-group collaboration.

> We'd love to collaborate with anyone that wants to collaborate with us. [But] Under the current research environment in China, I feel that our inner-institutional collaboration is more frequent than other kinds of collaborations. In other words, it's easier to work with other PIs within our own institution ... There might be two reasons that hindered communication between Chinese researchers within China. One is because everybody is busy, right? The second is precaution. This might not be too significant [a] factor, but it is one of my own concerns. ... There may be no mutual benefit ... We have tried to build up collaborations, but eventually they didn't work out. (Scientist 18)

Precaution against being taken advantage of and ensuring mutual benefits are undoubtedly universal rules in team communications. The difference lies in under what conditions and to what degree mutual benefits are acknowledged. What is interesting in Scientist 18's narrative is a delicate yet clear distinction between "precaution" in collaborating with distant groups and with groups in the same institution. This resonates with Lamont and Molnar's (2002) theory that symbolic social boundaries, such as professional affiliation, also generate a secondary social boundary which is "manifested in unequal access to unequal distributions of resources (material or nonmaterial) and social opportunities" (Lamont and Molnar 2002, p. 168). In the case of stem cell research, this means that the establishment of a new team not only marks a conceptual separation between one group of scientists and the rest, but also produces social boundaries, indicated by the extra "precaution" as regards distant groups. A simplified analogy may help to explain why the organization of scientists affects inter-team communication efficiency: if intra-institution groups have one boundary to cross (group A to group B), then the symbolic boundaries for external groups include several levels (group A to institution A to region A to region B to institution B to group B). All these social boundaries accumulate for potential collaborators to overcome. In other words, the Chinese team structure not only inhibits intra-group discussion but indirectly has negative effects on inter-group communicative efficiency as well.

In short, in the eyes of the interviewees, China's recent international recruitment of scientific talents seems to only satisfy one of the two necessary conditions in promoting China's research. Apart from generous funding programs, there also should be corresponding attentiveness to team-building. A common team structure found by this study echoes with OECD's description that China's life science system consists of a "very large number of 'innovative islands' with limited synergies between them" (OECD 2007b, p. 22). How flat team structures contributed to an over-dispersion of research resources and raised unnecessary communicative barriers are elucidated by the author's previous work (Zhang 2010b). This section, however, is to highlight the correlation between structural particularities and effective governance. The flat team structures affect research behaviors ("everybody is their own team-leader," Scientist 01), hamper intra-team coordination (PIs have "less commanding authority," Scientist 06), set actual research constraints ("however great your idea is, you have to start from scratch," Scientist 14; "precaution" against other institutions, Scientist 18) and result in a research environment with only host "sparks" of individual talents but no "intellectual deposits" (Scientist 31) to "set the prairie afire." To summarize, although China's stem cell governance exhibits generous financial commitments and an encouraging attitude towards world scientific excellence, its output seems to be curtailed at the grassroots level by team structures.

Regulatory institutions and macro-level inefficiency

Governing initiatives: collaborative governance?

At the onset of China's stem cell development a decade ago, ethical oversight was loosely carried out through local institutions. In the absence of a nationally recognized directive, skepticism arose internationally about the quality of Chinese laboratories' working standards and regulatory supervision. Stem cell research in China soon became a symbol for "a morally bankrupt 'Wild East' of biology" (Dennis 2002, p. 334). To enhance China's research credibility, MOH and MOST, the two main regulatory bodies concerning stem cell research, made a collaborative initiative and jointly promulgated the *Ethical guidelines for research on human embryonic stem cells* in 2003 (MOH and MOST 2003). At the time, this was seen as a major step for China to promote coordinated ethical governance across different institutions.

Fragmented administrative infrastructure

Before discussing the implementation of this regulatory initiative, let me first provide a brief account of China's administrative infrastructure. At the macro-level, regulatory responsibilities on stem cell research are divided among a number of national institutions, which enjoy similar legislative status. For example, MOH should "propose development plans for the state's key medical technology and education development, organize key medical and health research" (MOH Charter, www.moh.gov.cn). Stem cell research falls into this category. Meanwhile, MOST is commonly recognized as the principal mediator in China's scientific governance, "which supports big-ticket items and assists in the formulation of science and technology policy" (Ratchford and Blanpied 2008, 227). In general terms, MOH is a key player in setting medical-related research agendas, while MOST has both the regulatory authority and financial leverage in basic research.

The division of managerial accountabilities is not unique to China. In fact, with the complexity of stem cell research, many countries often assign administrative responsibilities to several regulatory bodies. For instance, in the UK, the issue of "processing stem cells" alone is divided into different processing stages and thus falls under the jurisdiction of two separate institutions: the Human Fertilization and Embryology Authority (HFEA) and the Human Tissue Authority (HTA). That is, the HFEA regulates the procurement of gametes up until the point where an embryo is created. Then, it is HFEA's remit to provide oversight on the use of embryos. Once the stem cell line is derived the HTA regulatory remit begins and the HFEA's regulatory remit ceases (Human Tissue Act 2007).

However, there is one major divergence between the British and Chinese arrangements of regulatory bodies. In the UK, both the HFEA and HTA work within the legislation reviewed and approved by Parliament, that is the Human Fertilisation and Embryology Act 1990 and the Human Tissue Act 2007. In China, the State Council's supposed role in cross-ministry coordination has so far only been nominal (Liu 2006), with different national agencies "independently formulat[ing] and implement[ing] their S&T plans" (Zhong and Yang 2007, p. 324). In other words, whereas in the UK, the division of administrative responsibility is based on cohesive decision-making with cross-institution overview, in China, the "current governance system" lacks the "interagency co-ordination to ensure the consistency and coherence of various policies" (OECD 2007b, p. 50).

MOH as the "mother-in-law"

Bearing in mind this fragmented characteristic of regulatory institutions, it may not be surprising to find that in practice, intended collaborative ethical oversight met with low compliance. Scientist 17 explained the situation as follows:

> [In practice] the Ethical Committee in MOH cannot supervise anything! One big problem is that MOH is not the money provider [so it has no say in funding decisions]. For example, in March 2007, one major reproductive center was to set up in Shanghai. The funder was MOST. So, the site inspection was hosted by MOST, I [an embryologist] was invited, a few Academicians were invited, but the Ethical Committee from MOH was not invited. [The actual relation between MOH and labs to be regulated is] like what local researchers say "MOH is just a mother-in-law. I won't let MOH cause us additional trouble." For example, if they [MOH] want to inspect my colleague's lab in Peking University, my colleague would tell the inspector, "sorry I don't want to be inspected" ... Researchers dare to do that because MOH doesn't exert influence over MOST's decision on their funding. (Scientist 17)

There are two points worth elucidating in this respondent's account. First, although MOH and MOST jointly endorsed the *Ethical guidelines*, there is not sufficient coordination in implementation. While both ministries employed inspection procedures to ensure decent research conduct, as each ministry had separate regulatory priorities, such inspection was carried out with different emphasis. As noted by this respondent, although MOST required compliance with basic ethical standards, its site inspection was mostly made up of scientific experts. This point echoes several accounts provided by ethicists:

> In terms of stem cell regulation, of course they [MOH and MOST] listen to experts' advice, but they only listen to those "hard-core experts" advice. I mean MOST only turns its ear to those scientists that work in the lab, MOST won't listen to us [ethicists]. (Ethicist 01)

> Probably it had to do with the nature of their job [priorities]: people from MOST were more inclined to listen to what the scientists say [while] MOH was a bit more cooperative [with us]. (Ethicist 02)

Secondly, as pointed out earlier, there is nothing essentially "wrong" with different ministries having different priorities. Yet what seems to have made MOH's regulation redundant was the fact that existing regulatory infrastructures posed a hindrance for the different priorities to be coordinated. As both ministries were entitled to decision-making autonomy, neither authority (MOH or MOST) can override the other's ruling on whether a particular research project should go ahead. Instead of providing complementary administrative support, regulatory rulings made by MOH and MOST became rivals. When conflicts arose, as demonstrated in the ethical inspection case given by Scientist 17, supposed joint supervision from MOH and MOST became local research groups' "pick-and-choose" on which ministry to follow. In extreme cases, as the example of Scientist 17's colleagues demonstrates, as long as they secure MOST's endorsement, scientists "dare to" ignore MOH's inspector by telling them, "sorry I don't want to be inspected." MOH is associated with a problematic image of a "mother-in-law." In other words, it was perceived as a non-directly (interests-) related superior who intervenes with research activities. Supposedly a main regulator in stem cell research, MOH became an "excessive" authority and its ethical guidelines "regulations-in-theory." Subsequently, the supposed collaborative ethical supervision was overshadowed by individual ministerial funding decisions.

The fragmented nature of regulatory authorities also offset potential assistance from scientists in achieving effective governance. One life scientist, who had been working in Nankai University for two decades, explained his indifference in shaping regulatory directives as follows:

> Every [administrative] office has their own standpoints, they have their own interests to take into consideration, so they view things differently from each other. I am not interested in making any suggestions to the current administrative system. No, no use ... they are neither going to listen to you nor listen to their peers in other

administrative branches . . . so what's the point of me wasting my time communicating with them? . . . I am not being cynical or anything. It's the system. If I were in their shoes, I'd think from my own point of view as well. Everybody take care of their own business, that's all. (Scientist 11)

This professor witnessed China's scientific reform in the past 20 years, and during the process was well connected with the scientific community in Tianjin. Yet, precisely because of his years of experience working as a scientist in China, this respondent deemed that the current governance initiatives made little difference in terms of actual governance efficiency, for one thing remained unchanged: the conventional administrative divide. In practice, as the decision-making authority and priorities in regulatory bodies were structurally independent from each other, administrators had little interest in incorporating wider concerns from researchers or "their peers in other administrative branches." Scientist 11 highlighted the seriousness of this structural limitation by stating that this was not a "cynical" opinion, but a matter-of-fact condition that would distort anyone's original objective if one "were in their shoes."

Similar to what has been demonstrated at the team level, at the ministerial level, many intended regulatory effects also fell short for they were discounted, offset, or even distorted, by the existing configuration among different administrative branches. The situation of China's stem cell research echoes Egeberg's (2003) findings on the connections between bureaucratic structures and policy implementation. That is, actors within an established ministry may be subject to particular moral and collegial pressures in challenging existing organizational incentives (such as narrow priority setting described by Ethicists 01 and 02) or amending institutionalized norms (such as uncoordinated site inspections described by Scientist 17). Thus, the reluctant "sympathy" Scientist 11 expressed towards regulators in different ministerial offices reflects Egeberg's argument that "structure can never be neutral," but always functions as a "filter" of potential alternatives and promotes certain actions (Egeberg 2003, p. 117). In other words, for a coordinated ethical governance to come into effect, MOH and MOST may need more than a joint promulgation of guidelines. They may also require corresponding structural adaptations in their jurisdictions.

Conclusion

In many ways China has been most diligent in employing new managerial leverages to promote effective scientific governance. Yet, "unsupportive framework conditions" and "insufficient interconnection among innovative systems" (Guinet and Zhang 2007) often weaken China's scientific initiatives. Despite generous institutional patronage, some have noted that "China does not yet have the infrastructure in place to fully take advantage of this increased spending" (Lane 2008, p. 256).

This article provides an empirical examination of how China's institutional structures influence effective governance. At the research team level, structural deficiency in retaining middle-layer researchers places practical constraints on the efforts of research personnel to fulfill national funding schemes' expectations. Similarly, managerial divides among national institutions also obstruct intended coordinative governance. When jurisdictions overlap, different social authorities may compete, diverge, or contradict in administrative judgments, which creates confusion and promotes inconsistency and minimal conformity with the law. This article is not aimed at proposing what an optimal regulatory institution structure should be, as this requires a separate investigation. It does however demonstrate that regulatory *structural* changes, especially in the case of Chinese stem cell research, should be regarded as vital as updating the managerial agenda in achieving effective governance. In all, just as a flat team structure cannot provide a sound "stage" for scientists to carry out their innovative ideas, the fragmentation of decision-making failed to enlighten a coordinated and well-balanced "platform" on which responsible research can efficiently proceed. Effective governance demands a parallel attentiveness to the structural organization of key stakeholders, such as scientists and regulators.

Acknowledgements

The author gratefully acknowledges the support of the Wellcome Trust Biomedical Ethics division who helped make this research possible through a PhD Studentship. I also wish to thank Dr Margaret Sleeboom-Faulkner and participants from "The social regulation of stem cell research: looking beyond regulatory exteriors in Asia" conference at the University of Sussex, who provided helpful comments.

Notes

1. For example, the Cross-Century Foundation for the Talents (MOE 1993), the Hundred Talents Program (CAS 1994), the Spring Bud Program (MOE 1996), and the Chang Jiang Scholars Program (MOE 1998) and the most recent "Thousand Talents Program" supported by a resolution promulgated by the General Office of Central Committee of the Communist Party of China (General Office of CCCPC 2009).
2. One team in Sun Yat-sen University, one in Nankai University, one in Chinese Academy of Sciences, one from Beijing Chinese Traditional Medicine Hospital and two from Peking University Health Science Centre.

References

Albert, E. and Mickan, S., 2003. Closing the gap and widening the scope: new directions for research capacity building in primary health care. *Australian Family Physician*, 32 (12), 1038–1040.

Burau, V., Wilsford, D., and France, G., 2009. Reforming medical governance in Europe. What is it about institutions? *Health Economics, Policy and Law*, 4, 265–281.

CAS (Chinese Academy of Sciences), 1994. *Director Lu Yongxiang's speech on 1994 Hundred Talents Program reporting conference.* Beijing: CAS. Available from: http://www.cas.cn/ggzy/rcpy/brjh/.

Chen, H.-D., 2009. Stem cell governance in China. from bench to bedside? *New Genetics and Society*, 28 (3), 762–282.

Cooke, J., 2005. A framework to evaluate research capacity building in health care. *BMC Family Practice*, 6, 44–54.

Corbin, J.M. and Strauss, A., 1990. Grounded theory research: procedures, canons, and evaluative criteria. *Qualitative Sociology*, 13, 3–21.

Corbyn, Z., 2008. China nears UK in brain games. The Times Higher Education, 7–13 August. p. 9.

Dennis, C., 2002. China: stem cells rise in the East. *Nature*, 419, 334–336.

DOH (Department of Health, UK), 2004. *Research capacity development strategy.* London: Department of Health.

DTI, 2004. *Stem cell mission to China, Singapore and South Korea.* London: Department of Trade and Industry, Global Watch Mission Report. Published online in January 2005.

Egeberg, M., 1999. The impact of bureaucratic structure on policy making. *Public Administration*, 77 (1), 155–170.

Egeberg, M., 2003. How bureaucratic structure matters: an organizational perspective. In: B.G. Peters and J. Pierre, eds. *Handbook of public administration.* London: Sage, 116–126.

Fox, C., 2007. *Cell of cells: the global race to capture and control the stem cell.* New York: W.W. Norton.

General Office of CCCPC (Central Committee of the Communist Party of China), 2009. *Central Government Personnel Work Coordination Committee's executive programs executive overseas high level personnel, 7* January. Beijing: General Office of CCCPC.

Guinet, J. and Zhang, G., 2007. OECD review of China's innovation system and policy: main findings. Paper presented at OECD-MOST joint conference: Review of China's national innovation system: domestic reform and global integration, 27August Beijing.

Hao, D.-F. and Liu, M., 2005. Research group management on basis of cohesive team structure. *China: Science and Technology Management Research*, 11, 87–89.

He, S.-G., 2008. Medical overseas-return's current situation and suggestions. *China Hospital Management*, 28 (5), 43–44.

Huang, C., Varum, C.A. and Gouveia, J.B. (2006). Scientific productivity paradox: the case of China's S&T system. *Scientometrics*, 69 (2), 449–473.

Katzenbach, J.R. and Smith, D.K., 1993. The discipline of teams. *Harvard Business Review*, 71, 111–120.

Lamont, M. and Molnar, V., 2002. The study of boundaries in the social sciences. *Annual Review of Sociology*, 28, 167–195.

Lane, N., 2008. US science and technology: an uncoordinated system that seems to work. *Technology in Society*, 30, 248–263.

Leibovitz, J., 2003. Institutional barriers to associative city-region governance: the politics of institution-building and economic governance in "Canada's technology triangle.". *Urban Studies*, 40 (13), 2613–2642.

Liu, H.-B., 2006. Analysis and suggestion on China's central and local political structure. *Internal Reference for Reform* [in Chinese], 6 [online]. Available from: http://www.iolaw.org.cn/showarticle.asp?id=2050 [Accessed 9 April 2011].

Magjuka, R.J. and Baldwin, T.T., 1991. Team-based employee involvement programs: effects of design and administration. *Personnel Psychology*, 44, 793–812.

MOE (*Ministry of Education,* China), 1993. *Proposed scheme for cross-century foundation for the talents,* October 1993. Beijing: MOE.

MOE (Ministry of Education, China), 1996. *"Spring Bud Program": rules on designated MOE's financial support on overseas personnel short term employment in China, 25* April. Beijing: MOE.

MOE (Ministry of Education, China), China, 1998. *Rules on the employment of Changjiang scholars in the "Chang Jiang Scholars and Innovative Team Program,"* 4 August. Beijing: MOE.

MOH (Ministry of Health, China) and MOST (Ministry of Science and Technology, China), 2003. *Ethical guidelines for research on human embryonic stem cells,* 24 December. Beijing: MOH and MOST.

Morgan, K., 1997. The learning region: institutions, innovation and regional renewal. *Regional Studies*, 31 (5), 491–503.

MOST (Ministry of Science and Technology, China), 2007. *Response to the proposal on encouraging overseas personnel leading national scientific research projects*, 3 March 2008, MOST Issue No. 603. See also http://www.most.gov.cn/ztzl/lhzt/lhzt2008/taya2008/ya2008/200803/t20080303_ 59448.htm [Accessed 9 April 2011].

Murray, F. and Spar, D., 2006. Bit player or powerhouse? China and stem-cell research. *New England Journal of Medicine*, 355 (12), 1191–1194.

OECD, 2007a. *Main science and technology indicators 2007/2*. Paris: OECD.

OECD, 2007b. OECD reviews of innovation policy: China. Synthesis report. *OECD in collaboration with the Ministry of Science and Technology China*. Paris: OECD.

Ratchford, J.T. and Blanpied, W.A., 2008. Path to the future for science and technology in China, India and the United States. *Technology in Society*, 30, 211–233.

Reagans, R. and McEvily, B., 2003. Network structure and knowledge transfer: the effects of cohesion and rage. *Administrative Science Quarterly*, 48 (2), 240–267.

Rey-Rocha, J., Martin-Sempere, M.J., and Garzon-Garcia, B., 2002. Research productivity of scientists in consolidated vs. non-consolidated teams: the case of Spanish university geologists. *Scientometrics*, 55 (1), 137–156.

Salter, B., Cooper, M., and Dickins, A., 2006. China and the global stem cell bioeconomy: an emerging political strategy? *Regenerative Medicine*, 1 (5), 671–683.

Salter, B. and Qiu, R.-Z., 2009. Bioethical governance and basic stem cell science: China and the global biomedicine economy. *Science and Public Policy*, 36 (1), 1–13.

Schaaper, M., 2009. Measuring China's innovation system: national specificities and international comparisons. OECD Directorate for Science, Technology and Industry Working Paper Series [online]. Available from: http://www.oecd.org/dataoecd/15/55/42003188.pdf [Accessed 9 April 2011].

Sleeboom-Faulkner, M. and Patra, P.K., 2008. The bioethical vacuum: national policies on human embryonic stem cell research in India and China. *Journal of International Biotechnology Law*, 5 (6), 221–234.

Solo, P. and Pressberg, G., 2007. *The promise and politics of stem cell research*. Westport, CT: Praeger.

State Council China, 2004 [2003]. The State's Decision on Further Strengthening Personnel Development Programs. Beijing: People's Press.

UKSCI (UK Stem Cell Intiative), 2005. UK Stem Cell Initiative, Global positions in stem cell research: China, 24 November 2005 [online]. Available from www.advisory_budies.dab.gov. uk/uksci/global/china.htm [Accessed 9 April 2009].

Wang, X. and Wang, W., 2006. Authorship distribution of stem cell publication on Medline. *Medical Information* [in Chinese], 19 (9), 1511–1514.

Wen, J.-B., 2007. Speech on the National Award Conference for Science and Technology, 27 February Beijing: Xinhua News Agency.

Zhang, J.Y., 2010a. The cosmopolitanization of science: experience from China's stem cell scientists. *Soziale Welt* [Special issue in English], 61, 255–274.

Zhang, J.Y., 2010b. The organization of scientists and its relation to scientific productivity: perceptions of Chinese stem cell researchers. *Biosocieties*, 5 (2), 219–235.

Zhong, X.-W. and Yang, X.-D., 2007. Science and technology policy reform and its impact on China's national innovation system. *Technology in Society*, 29, 317–325.

Zhu, Z.-Y. and Gong, X., 2008. Basic research: its impact on China's future. *Technology in Society*, 30, 293–298.

"Your problem is that your face reveals everything when you are lying": making and remaking of conduct in South Korean life sciences

Leo Kim

London School of Economics and Political Science, London, UK

In the emerging context of the knowledge economy, exploring how both the global economic environment and national context influence local research practices is of crucial importance. The Hwang scandal in South Korea illustrates a typical research practice geared towards the exploitation of labor and human resources in response to, and as part of, global competition in the life sciences. This article argues that the ongoing exploitation of young talent and labor in the Korean academic community, even after the scandal, represents the combined outcome of actors' interests, organizational power structures, and strategies of survival in a global knowledge system that constrains the conductivity of actors. Competition and exploitation are internalized in the self-governance of the life sciences, despite avowed commitments to more rational and democratic research practices at the institutional level.

Introduction

Much discussion has taken place on the regulative trajectories of stem cell research, both in Europe and in East Asia (Sleator 2000, Park 2004). An academic trend focusing on local particularities to explain different regulatory practices reflects the difficulty of reaching a global consensus on how best to guide research practice. In the case of East Asian countries, such as China and Korea, their cultures and status as "developing countries" are often quoted as undermining the effective regulation of stem cell research (Gottweiss and Triendle 2006), but little discussion takes place as to how different local cultures represent common global problems by which problematic cultural practices are reproduced.

This article argues that the emerging knowledge economy, which contributes not only to commercializing biotechnology research but also to the formation of micro-level human behavior, introduces a novel challenge to the effective regulation and sustainable governance of local research and research communities. While commercialization forces industry and academia to imitate each other's practices and organizational behaviors, it has been observed in the US biotechnology community that the convergence of research cultures exhibits an asymmetrical effect: whereas industrial researchers generally benefit from adopting a system that encourages academic autonomy and vibrant organizational cooperation, academics in universities generally lose their traditional autonomy and become more secretive and competitive, and less trustful of each other (Kleinman and Vallas 2006). This trend has also become an overwhelming problem in the Korean life sciences, although with some unique local manifestations.

The drive for commercialization in the knowledge economy undoubtedly provides an incentive for biotechnology research, especially in the industrial sector. In South Korea, however, scientific competition has mainly had negative effects on research communities. In South Korea, where the spirit of competition is emphasized without the necessary industrial–academic cohesion to support the research, fierce competition, especially in academia, has produced a vicious cycle of problematic scientific practices, such as fraud, coercion, and exploitation. This vicious cycle occurs in conjunction with individual actors' use of unsustainable survival strategies within this constrained environment. This problem continues to be observed in South Korea, even after the Hwang scandal.

The notorious 2005 Hwang scandal, involving the fabrication of experimental results and the coercion of junior female researchers to donate their oocytes, has inspired global reflection on the need for tighter ethical regulation of stem cell research. As I have argued elsewhere, Hwang and his colleagues' misconduct reflects many complex problems typical of South Korean society – one that leaves little room for spontaneous reflection on scientific practice and knowledge in general (L. Kim 2008). To further expand on the underlying influence of national culture, more explanation of the complex interactions of the Hwang scandal is required. Although culture itself is an important variable, the intersection of actors' interests, organizational power structures, and local strategies of socio-economic survival articulate national characteristics that are coupled with the global influence of the knowledge economy. The global mode of scientific production, micro-power relations between people and the way such power is exercised seem to reproduce Foucault's "conduct of conduct" (Dreyfus and Rabinow 1982) in the national context. As I demonstrate through a series of interviews, these variables shape and reshape local cultural characteristics.

By briefly reviewing the Hwang affair, as an introduction to my argument, I raise some new questions. Despite South Korea's successful transition from an authoritarian state to a democratic society over the last decades, why have many South Korean laboratories, including Hwang's, failed to establish a more democratic and rational research practice? Is the Hwang scandal merely representative of problems typically observed in "developing" countries? Or are there more fundamental, external factors related to global governance that significantly limit the choices available to individual actors and organizations? If so, what are the structural constraints, other than national and individual factors, that can be incorporated into a systematic reflection of both local and global stem cell research practices?

In an effort to answer these questions, I will review Hwang Woo-Suk's scientific experiments, explaining the structural constraints that eventually led to scientific disgrace. I argue that Hwang's case reflects the asymmetric effects of competition on institutions and actors in South Korea under the constraints of the global knowledge economy.

Research methods and data

To review Hwang Woo-Suk's trajectory, I researched his alliances with scientific actors during the critical 2004–2005 period. I interviewed the chief investigator who interrogated Hwang and researchers who were involved in the collaborative work. Social network analysis (SNA) was applied to map life scientists' social relations that represent collaborations among stem cell laboratories that received governmental grants under the 21st Century Frontier Project. The visualized results identify core actors in the network, and reveal their alliance strategies as well as the overall characteristic of the collaborative network (de Nooy *et al.* 2005). The raw data used for the network coding were collected from the official documents stored in KORDI (Korea Research and Development Integrative Management System) in November 2006. To trace the research environment after the scandal and to substantiate my findings, I also conducted an ethnographic study with students, researchers and stakeholders in the scientific field.

New challenges in the knowledge economy

While Hwang's celebrated image of Korean science and technology faded away after he was charged with fabricating stem cell experiments that shocked the global stem cell community, the Korean public's urge to support him remains intact. This supportive sentiment partly stems from the limitless pressure to compete in a globalizing world, as many Koreans have a fixed notion that science should serve as a vital instrument in carrying out the global economic struggle (L. Kim 2008, 2009). Although this phenomenon might appear to be a local representation of the generalizing term "bionationalism" (Gottweis and B. Kim 2009), neither "bio" nor "nationalism" is predominately reflected in the Korean public's reaction. For the concrete political–economic base of "bio" has yet to fully develop or integrate into Korean society, and rhetorical expressions of nationalism conceal individual motivations and desires lying behind ritualistic support for Hwang and his research, as they embody a sentiment of criticism and distrust of official institutions that have failed to deliver responsible accounts of science to the public (J. Kim 2009). Therefore, the term "bionationalism" is an overly generalizing term.

The new stem cell science, with its messiah-like promises for medical application and economic profit, provided the Korean people with hope and relief and
gave them confidence in a society fraught with competition. The typical attitude
in South Korea that regards science as an "economic engine" dates back to the
era of the developing state when Park Jung Hee's military regime rushed to indus-
trialize the country in the 1970s (H. Kim 2006). No wonder its legacy has had an
undeniable influence on the current role of the life sciences. But the sense of
urgency for a quick scientific solution, felt by scientists and lay people alike,
stemmed from the idea that the "knowledge economy" was essential for future
survival. Especially after the financial crisis in 1997, Korea promoted "venture
enterprises" to boost Korea's economy. The fortuitous "dot-com" boom helped
the Korean economy quickly recover in the early 2000s, but the market was
soon saturated and dominated by a few aggrandized IT companies. Subsequently,
the government designed its "National Basic Plan for Science and Technology
(2002–2006)." This scheme was inherited by the ascending Roh Moo Hyun
administration, which saw biotechnology as a promising "growth engine" for the
future economy, and used it to politically legitimize the new policy.

The nationwide aim to make science and technology lucrative, and therefore
"worthywhile," had a penetrating impact on academic life as well. Universities
were required to produce star scientists and exhibit concrete results for commercialization. So-called "neo-liberal reform" began to use quantified methods of evaluation to assess universities' and individuals' academic performance. Hence the
number of publications in reputable Science Citation Index journals became
crucial for scholars and universities, as academic promotion and education
budgets were to be decided on the basis of quantitative criteria. Universities also
rushed to adopt profit-making "spin-off" practices, resulting from the prevailing
belief that this trend reflected a zeitgeist for the orientation of academic knowledge,
which could be adapted to industrial needs.

By the middle of the decade, it became evident in South Korea that the codes and
practices of industry and academia in scientific research were increasingly traded
across the boundary between the two, stimulated by the urge to collaborate in an
effort to make scientific knowledge profitable. A few entrepreneurial scientists
could start their own business successfully by seizing an opportunity in the expanding biotechnology market. At the same time, a number of academics came to
experience intensifying competition and pressure to survive under the new evaluation system, inducing them to utilize whatever means and resources at their dispo-
sal to exploit the situation.

In addition to the challenges encountered in academia, the industrial sector in
South Korea remains fragile: there are still very few biotechnology firms that are
sizable and competent enough to guarantee successful, long-term research (Shin
2009). Compared to the economic success achieved in IT, biotech enterprises
require more starting capital and more enduring investment to be profitable.
Korean academics were noticeably overwhelmed by commercial and competitive

pressures, which in turn encouraged a labor-exploitative model in research and rent-seeking behaviors as a solution. In retrospect, Woo-Suk Hwang's laboratory and his collaborators represented a possible outcome of all these elements.

Scientific networks and structural constraints

Hwang's laboratory was well known for its massive size by the time he published his article in *Science*. It started with only five researchers in 1986, but increased to 23 by 1999, and finally became a "clone factory" with 60 employees by 2005. The main stimulus for this expansion was the news of cloning Dolly the sheep in 1998. After this groundbreaking news, many people immediately saw its future potential for applications of somatic cell nuclear transplantation (SCNT).

The main source of funding did not come from stem cell research grants until 2005, but came from the already established animal cloning technology supported by the government (G. Kim 2007, p. 139). Thus, the team had to appropriate other short-term grants, and make a strategic alliance with another group that had already been granted government funding for stem cell research, the medical team of Dr Shin-Yong Moon based at Seoul National University. As the Korean government applied a "select and focus" strategy to support profitable scientific research (L. Kim 2008), there was only one group that could secure a sizable grant for the project.

Hwang's team also had to rely on other experts from MizMedi hospital and Seoul National University medical teams for the derivation of stem cells. The contribution made by Hwang's own stem cell team, having a veterinary science background, was limited to the technical SCNR process, whereas other, unfamiliar, procedures, such as extracting the inner cell mass from the blastocyst and culturing stem cell lines, were left completely to two experts at the MizMedi hospital. Jong-Hyuk Park and Sun-Jong Kim, the two medical researchers, fabricated the experimental results in 2004 and 2005.

According to the prosecutor's report (Anon 2006), the main motive of the medical researcher's initial fabrication derived from the great pressure exerted by Hwang to produce results, and to derive cloned stem cells, as soon as possible. Sun-Jong Kim testified that he was skeptical whether it was feasible that the seeded blastocyst would grow to form a colony, so he mixed the inner cell mass with an embryonic stem cell clump brought from the MizMedi hospital. Kim reported to Hwang that he grew and derived embryonic stem cells from the inner cell mass, but the stem cell was the one brought from MizMedi.

Despite his groundbreaking "success" in 2004, Hwang was in a great rush to produce results as soon as possible, even if it meant fabricating them. While Hwang's personal ambition may be one reason for this, his structural location in the South Korean stem cell research community, as revealed in the social network analysis diagram, may provide another clue for a sociological explanation. Figures 1 and 2 illustrate the collaborative networks of stem cell researchers who

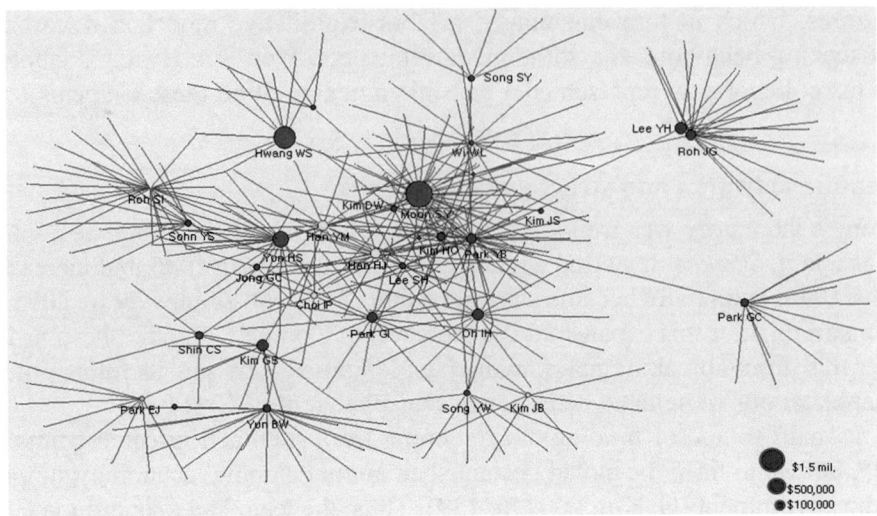

Figure 1. Stem cell network in 2004 (graphic produced and analyzed by Pajek). Notes: Red: Hwang and ally; blue: medical doctor; yellow: biology; green: bioethics (color online).

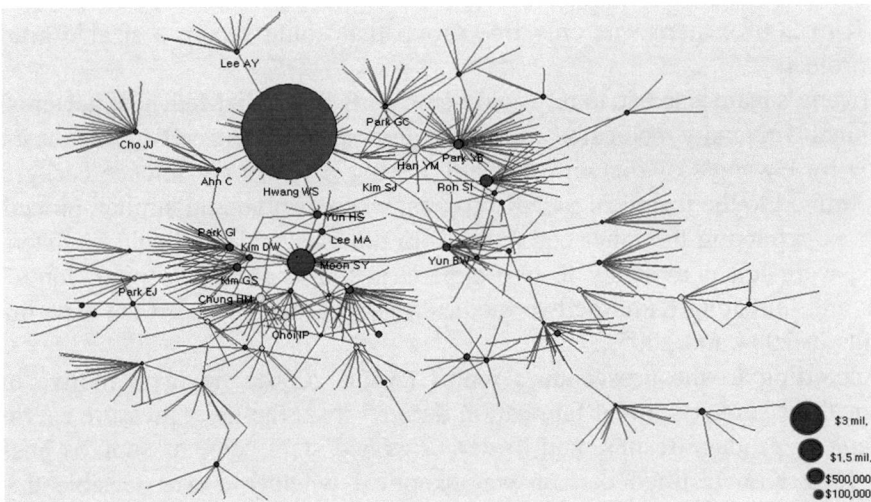

Figure 2. Stem cell network in 2005.

were granted governmental funding. As the main source of research funding comes from the South Korean government, these Figures reveal researchers' collaborative strategy and their structural location in the field that play a decisive role in the expert's career. As illustrated in Figure 1, Hwang's position is relatively marginal (or peripheral) to his ally Moon, who is positioned at the center of the network. At the time, Moon was the chief director of the Cell Application Project Team under the governmental 21st Century Frontier Entrepreneurial Scheme, so Hwang could secure his position only through the strategic ties made with him and Sung-Il Roh, the director of MizMedi hospital, who provided experimental staff and resources.

The situation noticeably changed in 2005, after Hwang acquired international fame by publishing his 2004 article in the journal *Science*. Hwang started to receive unprecedented amounts of research funding (see Figure 2). It also meant, however, that he had to legitimate his newly acquired status with new and better results. In the meantime, there was a growing tension between Hwang and Moon that led to them parting ways in 2004. According to Mr Park, the former chief of the National Board of Audit and Inspection that investigated Hwang prior to the prosecutor, it turns out that Moon's team made very little, if any, contribution to the research, though Moon listed himself as a corresponding author in the 2004 *Science* article. On the other hand, medical doctors in Moon's laboratory later complained to the auditing team that they were frustrated by Hwang's "greed," which would have led him to encroach upon their area of research: the derivation of stem cells. Hwang himself had to suffer the doctors' pejorative attitudes against him as a veterinary scientist and their uncooperative behavior during the research process (interview with the chief investigator, 28 May 2009).

The impending pressure for another breakthrough, especially after the cessation of cooperation from Moon's team, seems to have seriously affected Hwang's overall position in 2005. As clearly represented in Figure 3, Hwang's team had few external collaborators, and was isolated from the principal network led by the administrative figure Moon and the medical doctors. In order to overcome his precarious situation among his academic peers and to justify support from the government, Hwang used his personal capacity and position to make his junior researchers work even harder.

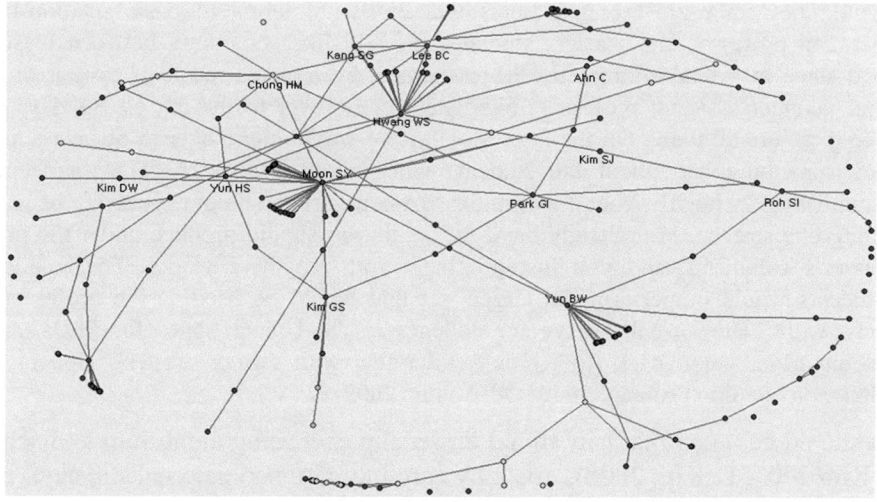

Figure 3. A bird-eye's view of the network in 2005.

Hwang's success in cloning a dog, which resulted in the puppy Snuppy, and his failure in human embryonic stem cell research, represent both the potential and the limitations of the labor-intensive strategy he adopted under constrained circumstances, that is, intensely competitive circumstances in which micro-strategies and resources as well as scientific achievements can play a key role. It appears that there have been two typical ways of acquiring competence in the new cloning technology over the last decade. One way was to improve the fundamental knowledge and techniques as Wilmut's team did in introducing the reprogramming method. The other was to mobilize a maximum number of human and material resources to produce greater outcomes, i.e. Hwang's hit or miss strategy. In a sense, his strategic choice was not only inevitable – because of the limited scientific foundations in South Korea – but it was also workable thanks to Korean researchers' highly disciplined work ethic and technical skills.

This competitive atmosphere contributed to the results-driven mobilization of labor and the cloning of Snuppy the dog that resulted from highly repetitive and arduous experimentation to imitate the actual process of conception, but was deprived of scientific inspiration and academic passion from the researchers. While admitting that Professor Hwang had the warm-hearted and admirable characteristics of a father, one of his postgraduate students still described his five years of laboratory life as: "the coldest days in my life; I was never more admonished or learnt more than in this period, in which I experienced the most gloom in my life" (G. Kim 2007, p. 135). A testimony from an interviewed graduate student in the College of Agriculture and Biosciences of SNU confirms that a similar research environment to that of Hwang's laboratory is widespread in ordinary academic life in South Korea:

> After the Hwang scandal, some changes were made in my department. For example, people now realize that they should keep experimental notes more accurately and would not embezzle research funds that easily. In terms of basic relationship between professor and masters students, it's still like something between master and slave in a feudal kingdom. Professors set the targeted result of experiments, and younger assistant professors alternately come over to the lab on Sundays to see if we are all there. On the next Monday, he would come over to our class and say something bad about the students who failed to turn up. That is deeply humiliating ... [sigh]. When I was in the MA course, I could not expect it to be anything like science. You already have the result you should produce under the professor's command, and you just go for it with repetitive works. The smartest students would outperform the targets set that would be used as the professor's own work. They usually leave for colleges in the United States for PhDs, and would never come back [to Korea]. (Interview with former master's student in SNU, on condition of anonymity, 30 August 2009)

It should be noted that patriarchal leadership exercising authoritarian discipline (G. Kim 2007, L. Kim 2008), offset by carefully rationed paternalistic care, is not unique to scientific research in South Korea. Rather, it is a typical form of "governmentality" (Foucault 1997) pervasive in society, which functions as an effective way to impose discipline, carry out exhaustive operations, and reduce internal tension with a symbolic attitude of paternalism that is "cheaper" than a system of formal reward and payment. Making potentially problematic conduct controllable, by force at first, and reconstructing the conduct as a sign of success, either through implicit recognition or through more concrete compensation, as Hwang and other academics did, appears to encourage the research actor's opportunistic behavior that is difficult to expose and check by formal institutional measures alone, as the following two cases demonstrate.

After the scandal: two cases

It is obvious that many problems were caused by local cultural practices and internal competition in Hwang's case. The traditional problem of lack of expert autonomy vis-à-vis institutional and bureaucratic influence (Bourdieu 2004) is also observed in the Korean scientific community more generally. As demonstrated in the following two cases, however, "local cultural practices," "internal competition" and the problem of "scientific autonomy" are becoming more deeply intertwined in today's mode of knowledge production. As the nature of what are "right" practices and "correct" knowledge are blurry and highly debatable in the life sciences, there is an incessant urge to make the most from the ambiguity. As Bernd Pulverer, chief editor of *Nature Cell Biology*, states, "99 per cent of articles submitted to scientific journals are somehow involved with beautification'" (Pulverer 2008). As the new entrepreneurial attitude among academics – one that is single-mindedly geared towards prevailing over competition – is adapted to and legitimized by the operation of the modern knowledge economy, it is extremely difficult for individuals to resist competitive pressures and the will to cheat for the sake of greater transparency. Compared to the "less modern" political dictatorship that had a visible, single center of power to resist against in South Korea decades ago, the implicit pressure of "economic considerations" is less visible but more pervasive in the country today. This new environment rewards submissiveness and punishes resistance to the prevailing, market-driven rationality in an invisible but more a sophisticated way.

Case 1

Jin-Yong (an alias) was a postdoctoral life scientist at the Korea Advanced Institute for Science and Technology (KAIST). He led major experiments in the neurochemistry department alongside his senior professor, and published first-authored articles in *Nature* and *Science*. By 2006, he was listed as one of the "100 most prospective young scientists" in the country. Then he accepted a fellowship in a high-ranked university in California. His successful career abruptly came to an end when a part of the experimental results he published in *Science* was questioned by the auditory body of the university. It was eventually exposed as a fabrication. It turned out that, although Jin-Yong had already brought about admirable achievements through the experiments, his professor had coerced him to exaggerate unproven results to augment the reputation of his venture business. Jin-Yong initially did not comply. But, faced with an outburst of furious admonishments, like those of a "mad man" according to his testimony, he finally gave in. Jin-Yong wrote in his statement:

> After the press interview announcing the experimental results [including the fabri-cated part], the professor told me, "Your problem is that your face reveals everything when you're lying [in the public announcement]. Look at Hwang. He was so confi-dent and sincere that at the brink of time [when] he was telling big lies, the public trusted him to the end! That is the capacity we need at this moment to win over the competition."[1]

Jin-Yong lost his PhD title in biology, and the professor was forced to resign.

Case 2

On 16 April 2009, the Parliamentary Life Science Research Forum organized a workshop in the parliament building to explore ways of promoting human embryo-nic stem cell research more actively in the future. This undoubtedly provided encouragement to many stem cell scientists in South Korea after the humiliating disgrace caused by the Hwang scandal. The underlying motives for this promotion were especially spurred by US President Obama's brisk move to lift former Presi-dent Bush's strict limits on embryonic stem cell research. South Korean policy on embryonic stem cell research, which had become strict, had to be reconsidered.

Dong-Wook Kim, chief of the National Stem Cell Research Center after Shin-Yong Moon's resignation, deplored the fact that Korea's position had been wea-kened over the previous few years by the "cynical atmosphere" following the Hwang scandal, and the subsequent withdrawal of government funding for stem cell research. Kim diagnosed that Korean scientists suffered from a "loss of war morale and ammunition." Another keynote speaker, Hyung-Min Chung, claimed that now it was time to move away from an "unproductive" debate on bioethics, and seek ways to respond to the rapidly changing international research situation. Clearly, there was a shared notion among speakers to regard the change in US policy as the "global" trend; there was also an atmosphere of shared irritation regarding ethical regulation in Europe. Eventually, Jung-Chan Rah, Director of venture cloning firm RNL Bio, asked: "Why does the EU raise bioethical issues while America is silent?"[2]

Discussion: the global knowledge economy and science

The South Korean experience in stem cell research reveals the difficulties encoun-tered in developing countries trying to simultaneously pursue the competitive application of scientific knowledge and the democratic governance of scientific practice. Sustainable governance of scientific research, including ethical regulation, presupposes a degree of regulative competence that is able to withstand the pressure of short-term interests, and a high level of basic scientific knowledge. Both elements also require sufficient economic and human resources to enable the implementation of long-term strategies. In that sense, it is conjectural that some leading South Korean stem cell scientists continue to rely on government funding, hard work, and a high number of biological resources, such as ova, for their ongoing research. In fact, a research culture that prioritizes an applied approach to science is the common reality for most East Asian countries. But the emerging local problems in the global knowledge economy can no longer be explained by national context alone.

Global norms for scientific conduct have yet to emerge. As observed in the UK, the effective alliance between policymakers who devise a permissive ethical regulative framework and the experts who are endowed with globally competitive knowledge can produce powerful global discourses for the governance of research. The regulative frameworks, such as the criterion of a 14-day limit on embryo research proposed by the Warnock Committee (see Jasanoff 2005), the endorsement of the "hybrid bill," and recent changes in egg donation policy in the UK clearly reveal that they are the institutional outcomes of the aims of policymakers, scientists, scientific knowledge, and strategies to legitimate a particular research process for national and social interests. In a similar vein, discussions on the ethical regulation of stem cell research are not independent of current modes of governance. Debates on ethical regulation can also contribute to competition through "defining power" (Beck 2009) and setting "global standards" that serve the political–economic interests of particular states. From a genealogical perspective, it is the nature of "neo-liberal governance" (Foucault 2008) to justify itself through the mobilization of discourses in pursuit of economic self-interest. Regarding the governance of stem cell research, we come to observe the same mechanism of legitimation. For the actors in the scientific field to reach a consensus on ethical regulations on a global level, it is important to realize that ethical governance should reflect the embedded "economic way of thinking and conduct" in human behavior as well as develop a common notion of bioethics. In this regard, deliberate efforts to provide economic incentives and social recognition to non-commercially oriented researchers can be as important as clarifying the boundaries of good research practice.

In this context, the definition of *ethical* requires a semantic extension that goes beyond checking for the fabrication of experiments or the institutionalization of bioethical procedures such as "informed consent" or the establishment of an institutional review board. These conventional ways of institutionalization do not problematize the global environment in which the majority of researchers are confronted with mounting pressures for survival, which may encourage scientific malpractice. The internalization of the logic of competition and the "asymmetrical convergence" of scientific practices between academia and industry are not just experienced as problematic for researchers in developing countries. Novel ways of creating a global "breathing space" that especially support junior researchers' individual autonomy, good research practices and international collaborations in science need to be discussed at a transnational level, and used to establish ethical commitments. As observed by Eriksson and Webster (2008), in their study of international cooperation in stem cell science, scientific communities can make concerted institutional efforts to invigorate basic scientific research on a transnational level. The international collaboration based on consensual ethical principles could also contribute to protecting the integrity of individual researchers and their rights as autonomous experts if the effort is effectively extended to the wider domains of scientific practice. Unless ethical considerations in science are extended to the core of the "conduct of conduct" to address the characteristics of the globalizing knowledge economy, the existing framework of regulation may at best externalize the modes of exploitation from wealthy countries to relatively peripheral, unwatched, countries. It is therefore important to find common pathways to reduce overall malpractice, which can be coupled with the current mode of global economic rationality practiced by the subject, rather than to simply blame local "cultures" for "underdeveloped" ethical governance.

Acknowledgements

I am immensely grateful to Margaret Sleeboom-Faulkner who provided remarkable support and demonstrated impressive leadership to make this research possible. I am also grateful to an anonymous reviewer and the Editor who showed strong trust in and support for my paper, despite a number of apparent flaws in my previous draft.

Notes

1. Jin-Yong's official statement presented to UCLA after the misconduct investigation.
2. Quotes are translated by the author. Source: International Institute for Asian Studies newletter

References

Anon., 2006. The prosecutor's report of the investigation of the Hwang case. Seoul: The Prosecutor's Office.
Beck, U., 2009. *World at risk*. Cambridge: Polity Press.
Bourdieu, P., 2004. *Science of science and reflexivity*. Chicago: University of Chicago Press.
de Nooy, W., Mrvar, A., and Batagelj, V., 2005. *Exploratory social network analysis with Pajek*. New York: Cambridge University Press.
Dreyfus, H. and Rabinow, P., 1982. *Foucault: beyond structuralism and hermeneutics*. Chicago: University of Chicago Press.
Eriksson, L. and Webster, A., 2008. Standardizing the unknown: practicable pluripotency as doable futures. *Science as Culture*, 17 (1), 57–69.
Foucault, M., 1997. *Il faut défendre la société. Cours au Collège de France 1976*. Paris: Gallimard/Seuil.

Foucault, M., 2008. *The birth of biopolitics*. London: Macmillan.

Gottweis, H. and Kim, B., 2009. Bionationalism, stem cells, BSE, and Web 2.0 in South Korea: toward the reconfiguration of biopolitics. *New Genetics and Society*, 28 (3), 223–239.

Gottweiss, H. and Triendle, R., 2006. Koreanische Träume. *Die Zeit*, 5 January.

Hwang, W-S. *et al.*, 2004. Evidence of a pluripotent human embryonic stem cell line derived from a cloned blastocyst. *Science*, 303(5664): 1669–1674.

Jasanoff, S., 2005. *Designs on nature*. Princeton, NJ: Princeton University Press.

Kim, G., 2007. *Hwang myth and South Korean science* [in Korean]. Seoul: Yukbi.

Kim, H., 2006. The present and future of South Korean society in view of the Hwang scandal [in Korean]. Paper presented at the Biotechnology Monitoring Conference, Seoul: South Korea.

Kim, J., 2009. Public feeling for science: The Hwang affair and Hwang supporters. *Public Understanding of Science* 18 (6): 670–686.

Kim, L., 2008. Explaining the Hwang scandal: national scientific culture and its global relevance. *Science as Culture*, 17 (4), 397–415.

Kim, L., 2009. Beyond Hwang "international stem cell war" in South Korea. *International Institute for Asian Studies Newsletter*, 52, p. 25.

Kleinman, D. and Vallas, S., 2006. Contradiction in convergence: universities and industry in the biotechnology field. *In*: S. Frickel and K. Moore, eds. *The new political sociology of science*. Wisconsin: University of Wisconsin Press, 35–62.

Park, E., ed., 2004. *Stem cell research ethic and legal policy* [in Korean]. Seoul: Ewha University Press.

Pulverer, B., 2008. Research misconduct: plagiarism, fraud and the integrity of science. Paper presented at the Wellcome Trust Workshop on Mechanisms of Fraud in Biomedical Research, 17–18 October, London.

Shin, J., 2009. *Eight Q&As in the biotech era*. Business report [in Korean]. Seoul: Mirae Asset.

Sleator, A., 2000. *Stem cell research and regulations under the Human Fertilisation and Embryology Act 1990*. Rev. ed. House of Commons Library Research Paper 00/93.

Regulating cell lives in Japan: avoiding scandal and sticking to nature

Margaret Sleeboom-Faulkner

Department of Anthropology, University of Sussex, Falmer, UK

The life sciences in Japan have been reappraised since late 2007 developments in human induced pluripotent stem (iPS) cell research. This article analyzes how Japan's research on fetal cells, human embryonic stem cells and iPS cells is co-produced with policies on funding, sourcing, bioethics, international regulation, and intensifying international competition. I argue, first, that regulation of human embryonic stem cell research (hESR) in Japan, though attempts have failed to engage the public, has been shaped through the leverage of social groups; and, second, that the 2007 reappraisal of hESR and the efforts made to advance to clinical applications in 2008 reflect a change in the orientation of policymakers toward regulation. Using anthropological notions of natural symbols, the article shows how the regulatory emphasis on what is regarded as ethical in the case of hESR has been confused with "safe" procedure, and how a risk-averse change in favor of iPS cell research according to stem cell scientists actually formed the reckless option.

Introduction

This article asks how regulation of human embryonic stem cell research (hESR) in Japan was shaped and how gametes, pluripotent cells and life values were embedded in discourses on procreation, including discussions on human embryonic stem cells (hESC) and induced pluripotent stem (iPS) cells. Because the former are sourced from embryos, and the latter created from somatic cells, hESC have been a source of contention in Japanese society, in contrast with iPS cells, which at the time were claimed to be identical to embryonic stem cells. The controversy around hESR led to a stringent regulatory regime for hESR, where regulation stipulates the respectful treatment of hESC as the "germ of life" (Sleeboom-Faulkner 2008). After the breakthrough in human iPS cells in 2007, a major shift took place in public opinion in favor of iPS cells, partly because iPS cells were seen as a product of Japanese science and partly because of their ethically uncontroversial nature compared to hESC (Editorial 2008, Liu 2008, Shineha *et al.* 2010).

Japan is often seen as an a-religious country, as historically it would never have attached great value to the "human rights" of the embryo or even a small child (Shimazono 2008, interview Shimazono 1). Nevertheless, Japan is crowded with religious notions and institutions, which express religious and spiritual concern. The newspapers expressed such concern:

> The creation of a legal framework in the form of a comprehensive basic law on bioethics in order to preserve the sanctity of life while not taking the edge off pioneering science is an urgent matter. (*Nikkei Shinbun* [Japan Financial Daily] 2002)

The question arises, then, of how the notion of the sanctity of life is related to the respect of pluripotent stem cells in a country that is widely advertised as being a-religious. In this article I argue that the context for the regulation of hESR in Japan is that of an ageing welfare society (see Moffett 2003, Masaki 2006), aiming to remain at the world's forefront in life sciences developments, while trying to cater for popular notions of Japanese culture.

Japanese policymakers have tried to open the way to human therapeutic cloning through the anti-cloning law (Kayukawa 2003) and by redefining the embryo as "the sprout of life." The power to "name" life here (de Certeau 1984) can be seen as the power to define what life means, who respects it, and who violates it. Defining what is respect for some forms of life, rather than others, and in which particular ways, rather than others, has enabled the regulation of hESR. Japan's history of eugenics, however, more crudely privileged certain forms of life over others, and, as explained below, has left widespread anxiety regarding reproductive technology, although feminists, democracy and human rights valorizations of life have steadily gained political weight. This article shows how contemporary policy making on stem cell research has largely been influenced by the historical symbolism of ethical concepts rooted in Japanese society, including the modern symbolism of "scientific advancement" and the natural symbolism of the embryo as "the sprout of life" and "respect for embryonic stem cells" (though not for iPS cells).

Japanese dominant discourses emphasize the importance of the notion of the group and symbols of nature, such as purity and danger (Valentine 1990). According to Mary Douglas (1992), symbols do not just dramatically express the social order and legitimize social functions, they are also modes of communication. In Japanese stem cell governance, rather than "rational" notions of scientific risk associated with the West (Beck 1992), it is the danger associated with scandal that the regulatory bureaucracy regards as a threat. In dominant discourses on Japaneseness (*Nihonjinron*) the violation of what is regarded as "natural behavior" through modernization and science and technology forms a menacing source of danger to Japanese culture (cf. Dale 1986, Sleeboom 2004, Robertson 2005). In short, political decision making around hESR is influenced by the perceived need of "scientific progress," and through socio-cultural notions of what is "natural" and "healthy" for society.

Natural symbolism is also relevant to understanding the strictness of regulatory implementation of hESR in Japan. Although audits and monitoring practices are important forms of social control in the Japanese life sciences, these notions cannot explain why the regulation of hESR became a sore issue in the halting field of hESR, in contrast with the immediate resolve to support regulatory leniency regarding iPS cell research. Other works have discussed pollution symbolism and boundary making in the context of safety and ethics in science research practices in laboratories (Franklin 2003, Wainwright *et al.* 2006, Sleeboom-Faulkner 2007, 2010a, Stephens *et al.* 2008). This article substantially extends these approaches by illustrating how natural symbolism and notions of danger in society have imbued science regulation and its implementation with emotional meaning.

This study draws on data gathered during 10 weeks of fieldwork in 2006 and six weeks in 2008 to gain insight into valuation of reproductive materials and potential scientific discoveries. The fieldwork consisted of archival research and semi-structured interviews with 40 stem cell scientists, 25 policymakers, students, eight housewives, and six religious professionals. The three latter groups were chosen to gain insight into the views of social groups, whose rough equivalents in Europe and the US object to hESR. Data obtained from interviews with stem cell scientists pertain to their views of regulation, its implementation, and public discussion, while data from interviews with students, housewives, and religious professionals served to obtain insight into popular understandings and support for embryo research and iPS cell research. Interviews with policymakers yielded insight into how various regulators and committee members deal with the diversity of public views and among scientists and with hESR regulation and its implementation. These data made the author aware that it was the fear of scandal and reputation blemish rather than the generally controversial nature of hESR that was problematic in the regulation of hESR in Japan.

Pseudonyms have been used so as not to attract attention to individuals, although none of the interviewees, when asked, expressed objections to being cited in articles. Interview questions concerned knowledge about, and the ethical issues of, regenerative medicine. In the case of scientists, they also included questions about the regulation of the research and work in the laboratory. Interviews took place mostly in the Kansai and the Kanto regions, where the main stem cell research (SCR) hubs are located, and interviewees were approached through contact networks, starting at the twelfth meeting for Genetic Engineering and Regenerative Medicine on 22 April 2006 in Kyoto. After sketching the historical background of abortion, and regenerative medicine, and summarizing official and public views on hESR and iPS cell research, the article analyzes the decision making underlying regulatory changes regarding hESR in Japan.

Bioethical confusion: regulating birth and lengthening life

In this section I argue that the bioethical confusion around embryo research in Japan needs to be, at least partly, understood in the historical context of both birth and ageing in Japan as a modern welfare state. A glimpse of Japan's eugenic history on abortion places the embryo in a clearer bioethical light. In Japan, induced abortion was not subject to prohibition until the Meiji reforms in 1868, when it became a criminal offence. In the 1930s, the eugenic law was introduced, making abortion a crime against Japan. It was relaxed in 1948 and, after the baby boom of the 1950s, abortion was allowed under various conditions. With Japan's modernization an alteration took place in Japan's family structure from the family household (*Ie*) to the nuclear family (small families, individualized decision making) (Matsubara 1998, Norgren 2001). From the 1990s, Japan's nuclear families were encouraged to give birth, and in vitro fertilization (IVF) became subsidized. In Japan's fast-ageing society of today the government and companies such as Matsushita financially encourage large families (Moffett 2003, Masaki 2006). In other words, a shift took place in the debate from a focus on the destruction of embryonic life (mass abortion) to an emphasis on the creation of embryos in a welfare society that is ageing and paying for families to have offspring.

Since the 1960s, contradictory trends in society, as a result of population policies, modernization and developments in reproductive technologies, complicated current discussion on the status of the embryo and abortion. First, though mass abortion takes place (over 300,000 induced abortions per annum), in principle induced abortion is still illegal under the penal code, which means that it has not yet been decriminalized. Since the 1970s, the increased abortion rate has been accompanied by the flourishing of *mizuko kuyo*, rituals for the spirits of aborted fetuses (LaFleur 1992, Hardacre 1997). Complex feelings about abortion and the taboo on discussing it openly kept most people out of the discussion. Second, the development of new reproductive technologies, such as IVF and intracytoplasmic sperm injection (ICSI) made artificial birth easier: currently over 1% of all newborns are brought into the world through IVF (Sato and Iwasawa 2006). But, although IVF aims to bring embryos to fruition, it also tends to destroy some in the process. Undergoing IVF, apart from being an emotional, financial and physical burden, raises difficult bioethical dilemmas: it requires potential parents both to highly value potential embryos and oocytes, and to be prepared to discard some at the same time. Third, at the level of society as a whole, although IVF adds some extremely desired members to the population, mass abortion seems to devalue embryos and fetuses of up to 12 weeks of age. The latter trend made possible the practice of using discarded embryos in research to find cures for diseases and issues related to an increasingly ageing population, a goal explicitly mentioned in the Millennium Project. In this context, scientists ask why strict guidelines on oocyte donation are needed if annually over 50,000 oocytes are being discarded.

But according to women's organizations such as *Soshiren*, these questions only add to the bioethical confusion around reproductive policy making and behavior (interview Nakauchi, 9 June 2006). This constellation of factors makes it hard to either fully support or reject research based on embryos.

This article argues that the bioethical confusion can be partly explained through the friction between conflicting notions of Japanese civilization, purity, naturalness, and the aversion to scandal, the adoption of pro-natal and ageing population policies, and a wish to be among the world's most advanced scientific powers. The friction between these notions has not led to widespread public engagement in the field of hESR. About a quarter of the interviewees – including scientists, housewives and policymakers in equal proportions – spontaneously noted in this context that Japan does not excel at holding bioethical debate.[1] The government, companies, communities and families, as a rule, are afraid of scandal. Japanese dominant discourse (*Nihonjinron*), which greatly emphasizes cleanliness and purity, ideologically rooted in its historical traditions, avoids reputational blemish and scandal (*omote*) (Valentine 1990). Talk about embryos remains taboo among the wider public, and procedures that deal with them are experienced as most sensitive.

Official stances on hESR

To stimulate economic activity after Japan's economic slump in the 1990s, the Japanese government set up the Millennium Project, a mega-project designed to encourage the innovation of science and technology, stressing the role of the life sciences. This political direction led to generous financial support for SCR in the universities. At the same time, much attention was paid to the regulation of bioethical issues associated with the research and applications in the life sciences. Rather than building regulation on "rational" categories of risk, regulatory authorities have been influenced by traditionally highly valued concepts of nature and the avoidance of scandal.

On 25 September 2001, Japan's Ministry of Education, Sports, Science and Technology (MEXT) under the Koizumi government implemented the decision to allow the creation of human embryonic stem (hES) cell lines for SCR. The research generated a bioethical need to redefine such embryos officially. A new concept of the embryo as the "germ of life" (*seimei no hooga*) was put forward, a notion that made respect for the embryo mandatory, especially among researchers in the laboratory (Kayukawa 2003, Morioka 2006). Simultaneously, it was decided to uphold the principles that the human embryo should not be created for research purposes and human embryos should not be destroyed for research purposes alone (cf. MEXT 2009). The new regulation allowed the isolation of hES cell lines in the Institute for Medical Frontiers in Kyoto, by Nakatsuji Norio and his team.

Only a few years later, in 2004, the Cabinet's Council for Science and Technology Policy (CSTP) voted for the use of hES cells from aborted fetuses in the laboratory and in clinical research. Its Bioethics Expert Panel decided to allow the creation of guidelines for therapeutic cloning, which were formulated in the *Interim Report Working Group of Therapeutic Cloning* in June 2006. Therapeutic cloning would only be allowed under strict conditions: only if the objective of research using hES cell lines was to cure serious diseases, and only if detailed informed consent procedures using a coordinator would be followed (Cyranoski 2005, Nakatsuji 2007). Furthermore, the donation of oocytes could only take place if derived from IVF treatment, frozen, or removed from the ovaries; the donation of somatic cells had to have guaranteed anonymity; the research institution in question had to have proven its high standards beforehand, such as having experience with animal cloning, hES cell derivation; it had to guarantee the participation of a researcher with experience in cloning primate embryos; and it had to apply appropriate ethical review. These conditions created a high threshold for candidate institutions to attempt therapeutic cloning. Even after three years, the Ministry of Health, Welfare and Labour (MoHWL) Committee for Human (somatic) Cloning in a Clinical Setting, led by Nakahata Tatsutoshi, found it impossible to develop regulation for the clinical application of hES cells: only for somatic stem cell research applications was regulation completed. One of the reasons for this was the scandal brought about by the discovery of fetuses among the refuse in Yokohama City Hospital (Yokohama Kokuritsu Byooin) (Sleeboom-Faulkner 2008), for subsequent surveys showed that similar practices were taking place in other hospitals in Japan. In short, the definition of the embryo as the "sprout of life," mandatory respect for the embryo, a meticulous implementation of the regulation by the bureaucracy, and a fear of public scandal turned hESR into a moral danger zone for scientists and regulators alike.

Public stances on hESR

In contrast to the impressions evoked by broad claims of the unity of the Japanese stance on bioethics (Robertson 2005), interviews revealed that Japanese views on the embryo, gametes and the fetus vary greatly. Views on the embryo range from regarding the embryo as the "germ of life" and the seed of life, to the embryo as sacred among Japanese sects. Views on the treatment of gametes include no objection to the donation of oocytes, a forbidding attitude to oocyte donation, and the attribution of *kokoro* or mind to ova (see also Sleeboom-Faulkner 2010b). Although many Japanese, in particular scientists, say that fetuses have no spirit, many women partake in ceremonies for deceased fetuses (*Mizuko kuyo*) (LaFleur 1992). But it is not entirely clear to what extent this means that women regard the fetus as having a spirit (Sleeboom-Faulkner 2010a).

The public discussion on hESR in Japan is limited (Kato 2005). Only the views of a few groups, such as the anti-eugenics network (which broke up in 2007), the *Soshiren* (Japanese women's movement), some patient movements, and religious groups were voiced in the media. Multiple positions on hESR coexist in Japan, varying from support for SCR to help handicapped people, support for SCR for infertility treatment, opposition to SCR when regarded as too artificial (*fuzhizen* [unnatural]) and too expensive, opposition to abortion and the interhuman transfer of biomaterials for religious reasons, and opposition to hESR as protest against the donation of reproductive materials by women (see Sleeboom-Faulkner 2008, Kato and Sleeboom-Faulkner 2009). But even though ample disagreement exists about hESR in Japanese society, and even though the government has invested heavily in national debate on the subject, public debate remained low key.

The low-key nature of the debate, according to group discussions held in December 2008, was due to the general aversion among Japanese people to "unnatural" practices and "high-tech" and "commercial" attitudes towards life, a view also voiced among some members of disabled movements (interview Chiba, 1 June 2006). Although approximately 30% of the interviewees viewed human fertilized eggs as "human lives," over 40% said that they would approve their use in research conducted to advance the medical science. What is regarded as problematic by most, however, is not so much the principle of using embryos or oocytes in research, but the idea of mainly focusing on high-tech methods for extending the lives of the ailing elderly, rather than improving the quality of life during the "natural" life span.[2] Another relevant point is that approximately half of the scientists (21) and nearly all non-scientists (25) said that the donation of reproductive materials should take place only to help kin. Potential donors also speak of the motive for embryo donation in terms of kin. Thus, research shows that couples asked to donate embryos usually respond in terms of "motherhood ethics" justifying the answer in terms of what is "best for the child" (Kato and Sleeboom-Faulkner 2011). The commercial incentives and the impersonal nature of the research were most mentioned as the reasons for the aversion (*kirai* [dislike]; *iya* [disgust]; *fushizen* [unnatural]; *ayashii* [dubious, suspicious]) felt against the use of reproductive materials in science applications. Central here then is the controversial nature of the disentanglement (Callon 1998) of reproductive material from the intimate sphere and its insertion into a commercial and impersonal economy.

IPS cells: bioethical relief and a boost to Japan's national pride

When Yamanaka Shinya and Kazutoshi Takahashi in 2006 published their research on iPS cells derived from mice, not many Japanese had heard of stem cells and pluripotency. In 2006, interviewees revealed that most laypeople had not heard of stem cells, though some could relate the subject to the Hwang Woo-Suk scandal around the fabrication of research data and unethical oocyte donation in South Korea (Sleeboom-Faulkner 2008). But according to a survey conducted by Shineha *et al.* (2010), over 80% of Japanese in 2008 had an opinion on regenerative medicine and expressed understanding of the significance of "pluripotency." Similarly, interviews I conducted indicated an almost universal awareness of the meaning of iPS cells and pluripotency among housewives and students.

Induced pluripotent stem cells (iPS cells) are products of the direct reprogramming of somatic cells to an embryonic-like state. This process involved the introduction of a limited set of transcription factors (initially four) and feeder culture (under ES cell conditions) to "fool" the somatic cell into reprogramming. Although Yamanaka and Takahashi, in October 2006, were the first to "discover" iPS cells, when they tried to apply their technique to human somatic cells, they had competition from Jaenisch's team of the Massachusetts Institute of Technology (MIT, USA), who published their laboratory's research results in the same month, in November 2007.

IPS cells discovery in Japan was received with great enthusiasm. It was front-page news for weeks, and was discussed in all newspapers, on TV and on the Internet. IPS cells were advertised as a bioethical cure for old-age diseases, not requiring oocytes or embryos. Compared to somatic cell nuclear transfer (SCNT), iPS cells promised to produce pluripotent cells with the same traits as human ES cells: pluripotency was the buzzword in the media. IPS cells were portrayed as an endless resource for producing healthy cells that could be used for clinical application. Also, in other respects, iPS cells compared favorably to other cells, as they occur in humans naturally (Nishikawa *et al.* 2008). The only problem – already on the way to being solved – was their tendency to produce teratomas, and the use of a viral vector. Using fewer and other genetic factors and finding an alternative to viral vectors were to solve these problems.

Much was made of Yamanaka as the "good" scientist, who persevered in his quest to generate new medicines, spinning out Yamanaka's narrative that once it had occurred to him that the embryo he saw in a friend's lab through a microscope could have been like one of his daughters (interview 6 May 2006). When there was talk of the clinical application of iPS cells, the press quoted Yamanaka as saying that the simplicity of iPS cells warranted regulation, as in the near future anyone would be able to create them, including iPS cells that could be developed into gametes (Alford 2008, Anon 2008). The speed with which government support was mobilized for the new scientific discovery was unprecedented (interview Sato 17 March 2008). Prime Minister Fukuda, then the chair of the Cabinet's Council for Science and Technology Policy (CSTP, *Kagaku Sogo Kenkyukai*), ordered an urgent policy review, and MEXT immediately started developing policies to regulate iPS cell research and its future applications. Meetings with civil servants and scientists were promptly organized the month after Yamanaka and Takahashi's article was published in *Cell*, and by 22 December 2007 MEXT had made plans to raise the funding on iPS cell research from 270 million yen (US$2.5 million) for research in 2007, to 2.2 billion yen for the 2008 fiscal year, pledging 10 billion yen over the next five years (Cyranoski 2008). Half of the 2.2 billion yen was to be pumped into Yamanaka's iPS cell research to be housed in a new institute for iPS cell research at Kyoto University in the new national center, the Institute for Integrated Cell-Material Sciences (iCeMS). Furthermore, the MoHLW would channel close to 100 million yen in the 2008 fiscal year directly to Dr Yamanaka, in addition to 410 million yen for regenerative medicine infrastructure, such as a cell-processing center (Cyranoski 2008).

This move was made not just because research on pluripotency was no longer to be obstructed by bioethical hurdles, but also because many scientists, including Nakauchi Hiromitsu, Chairman of the Japanese Society for Regenerative Medicine (JSRM), pointed out that other countries could win the competition for medical applications and patents (see http://www.jsrm.jp/index.html). This concern was expressed in the regulation of the Japan Science and Technology Agency, which emphasized the need for paying attention to competition, the nature of patent acquisition and bioethical appropriateness (JSTA 2009).

But the majority of interviewed scientists in various fields of SCR (30 = 75%), when asked for their view on current policies on the allocation of science resources, doubted the wisdom of the government's heavy investment in iPS cell research. They argued that if one wants to cure diseases such as Alzheimer's or Parkinson's, a "rational" approach requires one to try out various possibilities: using different methods and different cells, comparing the success rates of fetal cells, hESR through SCNT and iPS cells. At present, they argue, it is not yet clear if any cell therapy works. And, if it does, it is not known which is most effective, and which is safest. However, the situation in Japan was not conducive to such a diversified approach.

Regulatory ambiguity: between permissiveness and ethicality

The disagreement in Japan about priorities in regenerative medicine is apparent in the development of bioethical regulation. An officially permissive approach permitted hESR to conduct research aiming to cure serious diseases, guiding the creation of hES cell lines and "special embryos" (*toku teihai*), while the urgency of regulating "therapeutic cloning" and iPS cell research to advancing research was recognized. But this permissive attitude was overshadowed by a bureaucratic approach to hESR. Complex procedures for both establishing ES cell lines and their use involving double-review by the institutional review board (IRB) and MEXT could take over a year (Nakatsuji 2007), while changes in protocol or research team required additional applications. Special equipment was required for storing and discarding hES cells, e.g. a furnace, and a room exclusively used for hES cells. Thus hES cell lines could not be stored in the same room as animal cells, even though they were maintained by animal (mouse) feeder. Ordinary hES cells then are to be respected, while their supposedly identical iPS cell counterparts did not receive any such treatment. Thus, the permissive approach aimed at advancing hESR was countered by a purist approach adopted by the regulatory bureaucracy, whose accountability for ethical research makes it responsible for improprieties and scandal.

The bureaucratic approach is informed by a circumspect attitude towards propriety. According to cell banker Murakami, civil servants run the risk of losing their jobs or of being sued if they are seen to be inappropriately backing fetal stem cell research or gene therapy, or allowing hESR without the utmost scrutiny. Gene therapy trials in Japan, according to fetal scientist Kawahara, are usually only attempted when American and European research has shown it is "safe." Guidelines issued in the spring of 2006 stipulated that oocyte donation informed-consent procedures are only put in place when primate somatic cell nuclear transfer (SCNT) has been shown to be possible, or when human SCNT has succeeded abroad. These conditions took into account the increasingly louder views of feminist and disabled movements who stand up for the position of women; and took into account paternalistic attitudes associated with Japanese doctors and a growing distrust among the public of scientists' "Western" and "rational" approaches towards medicine, which are blamed for losing the "Japanese" human factor essential to a society plagued by suicides and an increase in "un-Japanese" practices such as using "brain death" as a criterion for pronouncing death, "euthanasia" and prenatal testing (Morioka 1995, Lock 2002, Tsuge 2010).

Ethical, reckless and scientific research

This section shows how the distinction between ethical, reckless and scientific research facilitates the understanding of Japan's policy turnaround in 2007–2008. Reliance on compromises between permissive and purist approaches created friction among policymakers, scientists and social movements, which was lessened by the discovery of iPS cells. The enormous attention given to iPS cells in late 2007 resulted from the relief of not having to deal with the thorny bioethical issues around embryo research in a field in which Japan had taken the global lead. The media speculated on the possibilities of using iPS cells in regenerative therapies without the problems of immune reaction and ethical dilemmas associated with oocyte and embryo donation. In December 2007, it was decided to invest substantially in iPS cells development and therapies, mainly institutionalized in the Center for iPS Cell Research and Application (CiRa) and the Institute for Integrated Cell-Material Sciences (iCeMS) in Kyoto University, and to speed up the development of iPS cells and patent law concentrated in Kyoto. At the beginning of 2008, the creation of so-called "*Suupaa Tokku*" – special research fields, such as for iPS cell research and hESR, organized around licensed research institutions – was designed to speed up the review of research proposals and the development of protocol (see Kitagawa and Woolgar 2008). A special task force from MEXT allowed therapeutic cloning in December 2007 (MEXT 2008), and in October 2008 various scientists expressed the belief that rules regarding oocyte donation would become less stringent in the near future (regulated in MEXT 2009). In October 2008, it was decided to loosen regulation around the application for hES cell lines (regulated in MEXT 2009),[3] and in November 2008 the ethics committee of the CSTS allowed the creation of gametes from pluripotent cells.

Contrary to expectations, the majority of interviewed scientists regarded as "reckless" (*musekinin*) the radical switch in research emphasis from a purist and strictly regulated hESR regime to a bioethically correct but unregulated iPS cell research regime in late 2007.[4] Pluripotent cells created from iPS cells were presented as identical to hES cells, even though scientists in Japan and in the USA commented on the limited available knowledge about the molecular processes underlying the reprogramming of somatic cells involving iPS cells. Nor had iPS cells been directed to differentiate into specific functional tissues or organs. And although alternatives to the use of teratoma-generating retroviruses were being sought, the introduction of genetic factors still meant that genetic alteration could take place, the consequences of which were hard to gauge. Thus, there was not yet confirmation of a genetic identity between the cell type generated from iPS cells and that of the patient. And, according to all interviewed stem cell scientists, the behavior of iPS cells and their therapeutic effectiveness depends on the environment in which the cells are going to end up. Concentrating on iPS cell research at the expense of other branches of SCR, according to most scientists, was a risky strategy: it threatened the loss of current expertise and it was based on unexplored presumptions about the nature of iPS cells.

Discussion

Bioethical regulation of hESR in the UK has been cited as rooted in public opinion, exemplified by the engagement of the public in debates on embryo and oocyte donation (Human Fertilisation and Embryology Authority: http://www.hfea.gov.uk/consultations/index.jsp). Developments in the Japanese governance of hESR show how regulation can be rooted in society differently. Although its public engagement strategy received little public response (Kato 2005), Japan's stem cell regulation was nevertheless largely steered by society. For, although the state adopted a permissive political stance towards hESR, its regulatory practice largely relied on the opinions of particular social groups. In accordance with Douglas' notion of "group," public communication and views on regulation were influenced by natural symbols linked to danger rather than based on risk calculations. Japan's regulation and its implementation in the case of hESR was conditioned by a fear of scandal, while popular opinion was led by symbolic notions of what counts as "natural" reproduction and personal care in the context of the family. Thus, most of those in favor of oocyte and embryo donation described it in terms of helping a family member rather than as something that can be done on a large scale for public purpose (such as blood donation) or something that can become part of a commercial economy to help the ageing. IPS cell research on the other hand became associated with the possibility of wide commercial distribution and large-scale application in regenerative medicine. In 2008 there was little sign that iPS cell research would receive the same scrutiny as that to which hESR had been subject. Even though the adherence to existing ethical research regulation may formally determine whether science research is ethical, the mode of its creation and implementation was influenced by the societal environment. In Japan, hESR regulation was influenced through group symbols of ethicality, while their absence in the case of iPS cell research made it relatively insensitive to questions of risk in a similar research field. The resultant "recklessness," a majority of interviewed stem cell researchers found equally damaging to scientific advancement.

Notes

1. In fact, extensive debate has been held on other bioethical topics, such as euthanasia, eugenics and surrogacy.
2. Similar views were obtained by Tsuge (2008); also see Lock (1998).
3. MEXT revised its guidance for human ES cells research (effective from 21 August 2009) by omitting the review by MEXT and easing the regulation for transferring cells created from human ES cells among research institutions (see http://ukinjapan.fco.gov.uk/resources/en/pdf/ 5606773/200908news).
4. Even the wider public in support of iPS cell research desired international regulation and restraint (Shineha *et al.* 2010).

References

Alford, P., 2008. Japan's stem cell research surge. *The Australian*, 19 January [online]. Available from: http://www.theaustralian.news.com.au/story/0,25197,23073347-23850,00.html [Accessed 30 June 2011].

Anon, 2008. Japanese scientist says regulations needed for non-embryo stem cells to avoid abuse. *International Herald Tribune*, 9 January, p. 9.

Beck, U., 1992. *Risk society: towards a new modernity.* London: Sage.

Callon, M., 1998. Introduction: the embeddedness of economic markets in economics. *In*: M. Callon, ed. *The laws of the markets.* Oxford: Blackwell, 1–57.

Cyranoski, D., 2005. Japan's embryo experts beg for faster ethical reviews. *Nature*, 438 (7066), 263.

Cyranoski, D., 2008. Stem cells: a national project. *Nature*, 451 (7176), 229.

Dale, P., 1986. *The myth of Japanese uniqueness.* London: Routledge.

de Certeau, M., 1984. *The practice of everyday life.* Berkeley: University of California Press.

Douglas, M., 1992. *Natural symbols.* London: Routledge.

Editorial, 2008. *Mainichi Xinbun*, 7 March, p. 3.

Franklin, S., 2003. Ethical biocapital: new strategies of cell culture. *In*: S. Franklin and M. Lock, eds. *Remaking life and death: toward an anthropology of the biosciences.* Oxford: James Currey, 97–127.

Hardacre, H., 1997. *Marketing the menacing fetus in Japan.* Berkeley: University of California Press.

JSTA (Japan Science and Technology Agency), 2009. *Strategic sector: "creating fundamental technologies for advanced medicine through generation and regulation of stem cells, based on cellular reprogramming"* [online]. Available from: http://www.jst.go.jp/kisoken/teian/en/mokuhyo/ h20-ips.html. [Accessed 30 June 2011].

Kato, K., 2005. The ethical and political discussions on stem cell research in Japan. *In*: W. Bender, C. Hauskeller and A. Mauzei, eds. *Grenzüberschreitungen* [Crossing borders]. Münster: Agenda Verlag, 369–382.

Kato, M. and Sleeboom-Faulkner, M., 2009. Culture of marriage, reproduction and genetic testing in Japan. *Biosocieties*, 4 (2–3), 115–127.

Kato, M. and Sleeboom-Faulkner, M., 2011. Meanings of the embryo in Japan: narratives of IVF experience and embryo ownership. *Sociology of Health & Illness*, 33 (3), 434–447.

Kayukawa, J., 2003. *Kuroun Ningen* [Human cloning]. Tokyo: Koubunsha Shinsho.

Kitagawa, F. and Woolgar, L., 2008. Regionalisation of innovation policies and new university–industry links in Japan: policy review and new trends. *Prometheus*, 26 (1), 55–67.

LaFleur, W., 1992. *Liquid life: abortion and Buddhism in Japan*. Princeton, NJ: Princeton University Press.

Liu, S.V., 2008. Towards a balanced view on iPS cells. *Local Biology*, 8 (1), 32–38.

Lock, M., 1998. Perfecting society: reproductive technologies, genetic testing, and the planned family in Japan. *In*: M. Lock and P. Kaufert, eds. *Pragmatic women and body politics*. Cambridge: Cambridge University Press, 206–219.

Lock, M., 2002. *Twice dead: organ transplants and the reinvention of death*. Berkeley: University of California Press.

Masaki, H., 2006. Japan stares into a demographic abyss. *Asian Times*, 9 May [online]. Available from: http://www.atimes.com/atimes/Japan/HE09Dh04.html [Accessed 30 June 2011].

Matsubara, Y., 1998. The enactment of Japan's sterilization laws in the 1940s: a prelude to postwar eugenic policy. *Historia Scientiarum*, 8 (2), 87–201.

MEXT, 2008. *Regulation for therapeutic cloning for research purposes*, 1 February [online]. Available from: http://www.lifescience.mext.go.jp/files/pdf/2_32.pdf [Accessed 30 June 2011].

MEXT, 2009. *Guidelines for the establishment and utilization of human embryonic stem cell lines*, 20 May [online]. Available from: http://www.lifescience.mext.go.jp/files/pdf/55_223.pdf [Accessed 30 June 2011].

Moffett, S., 2003. For ailing Japan, longevity begins to take its toll. *The Wall Street Journal*, 11 February p. A1.

Morioka, M., 1995. Bioethics and Japanese culture: brain death, patients' rights, and cultural factors. *Eubios Journal of Asian and International Bioethics*, 5, 87–91 [online]. Available from: http://www.eubios.info/EJAIB54.htm [Accessed 30 June 2011].

Morioka, M., 2006. The ethics of human cloning and the sprout of human life. *In*: H. Roetz, ed. *Cross-cultural issues in bioethics: the example of human cloning*. Amsterdam: Rodopi, 1–16.

Nakatsuji, N., 2007. Irrational Japanese regulations hinder human embryonic stem cell research. *Nature Reports Stem Cells*, 9 August [online]. Available from: http://www.nature.com/stemcells/2007/0708/070809/full/stemcells.2007.66.html [Accessed 30 June 2011].

Nihon Keizai Shinbun [Japan Financial Daily], Editorial, 25 June 2002. p. 12.

Nishikawa, S.-I., Goldstein, R., and Nierras, C.R., 2008. The promise of human induced pluripotent stem cells for research and therapy. *Nature Reviews Molecular Cell Biology*, 9 (9), 725–729.

Norgren, T., 2001. *Abortion before birth control: the politics of reproduction in postwar Japan*. Princeton, NJ: Princeton University Press.

Robertson, J., 2005. Dehistoricizing history: the ethical dilemma of "East Asian bioethics." *Critical Asian Studies*, 37 (2), 233–250.

Sato, R. and Iwasawa, M., 2006. Contraceptive use and induced abortion in Japan: how is it so unique among the developed countries? *Japanese Journal of Population*, 4 (1), 33–54.

Shimazono, S., 2008. Why must we be prudent in research using human embryos: differing views of human dignity. *In*: W.R. LaFleur, G. Boehme and S. Shimazono, eds. *Dark medicine*. Bloomington: Indiana University Press, 201–222.

Shineha, R., *et al.*, 2010. Familiarity and prudence of the Japanese public with research into induced pluripotent stem cells, and their desire for its proper regulation. *Stem Cell Reviews and Reports*, 6 (1), 1–7.

Sleeboom, M., 2004. *Academic nations in China and Japan: framed by concepts of nature, culture and the universal*. London: Routledge/Curzon.

Sleeboom-Faulkner, M., 2007. Regulating "respect for the embryo in Japan." Paper presented at the Conference on Governing Genomics: Interdisciplinary Perspective on the Regulation of the Biosciences, 25–27 January, ESRC Centre for Genomics in Science, University of Exeter.

Sleeboom-Faulkner, M., 2008. Claiming the futures of human embryonic stem cell research in Japan: minority voices and their amplifiers. *Science as Culture*, 17 (1), 95–97.

Sleeboom-Faulkner, M., 2010a. Boundary-making between science, society and the world: the case of stem cell research in China. *East Asian Journal for Science, Technology and Society*, (EASTS), 4 (1), 31–51.

Sleeboom-Faulkner, M., 2010b. Contested embryonic culture in Japan – public discussion, and human embryonic stem cell research in an aging welfare society. *Medical Anthropology*, 29 (1), 44–70.

Stephens, N., Atkinson, P., and Glasner, P., 2008. The UK Stem Cell Bank as performative architecture. *New Genetics and Society*, 27, 87–99.

Takahashi, K. and Yamanaka, S. 2006. Induction of pluripotent stem cells from mouse embryonic and adult fibroblast cultures by defined factors. *Cell*, 126(4), 663–676.

Tsuge, A., 2008. Can iPS cells break through contradictions in Japan? Paper presented at the Conference on the Social Regulation of Stem Cell Research: Looking beyond Regulatory Exteriors in Asia, 15 December, University of Sussex, Falmer.

Tsuge, A., 2010. How Japanese women narrate their experiences of prenatal testing: ultrasound, maternal serum screening, and amniocentesis. *In*: M. Sleeboom-Faulkner, ed. *Frameworks of choice: prenatal and genetic testing in Asia*. Amsterdam: University of Amsterdam Press, 109–123.

Valentine, J., 1990. On the borderlines: the significance of marginality in Japanese society. *In*: E. Ben-ari, B. Moeran and J. Valentine, eds. *Unwrapping Japan*. Manchester: Manchester University Press, 36–57.

Wainwright, S.P., *et al.*, 2006. Ethical boundary-work in the embryonic stem cell laboratory. *Sociology of Health & Illness*, 28 (6), 732–748.

Reconsidering ethical issues about "voluntary egg donors" in Hwang's case in global context

Azumi Tsuge and Hyunsoo Hong

Department of Sociology, Meijigakuin University, Tokyo, Japan

In the scandal around Korean stem cell scientist Woo-Suk Hwang, the inappropriate collection of human eggs as research material, fabricated data on ES cells obtained through somatic cell nuclear transfer, and fraudulent fundraising were condemned as legal and ethical transgressions. Among the criticisms, the donation of eggs by many women became a big issue. Some of the women were motivated by financial compensation or in-kind support, while others decided to donate their eggs without payment, being convinced that the research would bring therapy for thus far incurable patients, a promise unfulfilled. Regardless of the multiple reports published to articulate why the Hwang scandal happened in South Korea, we realized during our ethnographical fieldwork in that country that it would be meaningful to consider the ethical issues in a global context. In this paper, we focus on the motivations of the South Korean women who donated their eggs voluntarily as research materials, and aim to understand it in a more general context. We point out that not only their love of family but also other altruistic motivations for donating eggs are affected by the attitudes revealed in their narratives. Finally, we argue that there is a serious bioethical issue when a social environment of sick or disabled people makes women decide to help these individuals by donating eggs.

Introduction

After human induced pluripotent stem (iPS) cells were produced in 2008, politicians, the media, and religious leaders became enthusiastic about iPS cell research as a potential way for avoiding the ethical issues surrounding embryonic stem (ES) cells with somatic cell nuclear transfer (SCNT), which requires either human embryos or eggs as research materials. The immense admiration for iPS cell research seems to have been affected by the Woo-Suk Hwang scandal in South Korea. Hwang was a leading scientist in the field of human ES cell research and SCNT who rose to the top after publishing two papers in relation to human ES-SCNT in *Science* in 2004 and 2005 (Hwang *et al.* 2004, 2005). However, these two papers involved not only a serious violation of medical ethics in collecting human eggs but also fabrications and falsifications of scientific data (Hong 2008, p. 2).

Before the scandal was exposed, Hwang emphasized in an interview that "the Korean egg donors were not paid and were motivated by a desire to help sick people and national pride" (Cyranoski 2004a, p. 14). After the interview, an ethical problem involving egg donation by two junior researchers in his team was pointed out (Cyranoski 2004b). In addition, a Korean TV program aired doubts about the existing payments to egg donors for Hwang's team, which violated the Bioethics and Safety Law issued in 2005. Soon after the exposure of the egg trade, Hwang admitted inappropriate egg acquisition by his research team and apologized in public. This, however, led to the disclosure of data fabrication in his two papers.

According to the National Bioethics Committee of South Korea, which surveyed the inappropriate egg donation and data fabrication by Hwang's team, the team received a total of 2221 eggs from 119 women; 63 women had provided their eggs as a "commercial donation," 22 as "donation with in-kind benefit," and 34 as "voluntary donation" including two researchers in Hwang's team (National Bioethics Committee 2006, pp. 4–9). The case of the women who underwent their fertility treatment and gave their eggs for Hwang's research with their treatment cost reduced was categorized as "donation with in-kind benefit."

While "commercial donation" or "donation with in-kind benefit" was considered as compelling motivation, "voluntary donation" made by 34 females, including two researchers, caused doubts about their motivation. The information provided to those women, claiming that donated eggs would be used for therapy for people suffering from intractable illnesses and disabilities, strongly influenced and persuaded the women to donate their eggs (Myung 2006). According to anthropologist Y.G. Paik, family planning led by the Korean government in the 1970s raised women's consciousness about their bodies (Paik 2006). In an analysis by Leem and Park it was suggested that present-day reproductive technologies and cosmetic surgery have made Korean women aware of their right to dispose of their body parts, which encouraged those women to donate their eggs to Hwang's research (Leem and Park 2008).

These Korean studies depict in detail the complexity of the Hwang affair and its implicit background. But an emphasis on the distinctive factors in Korea might give the impression that lessons learnt from the affair inside South Korea are not useful outside it. Therefore we examine issues of egg donation conjunctively in South Korea and in a global context. Thus, we compare voluntary egg donation to Hwang's team with egg donation in other countries, using data for which we conducted interviews or archival studies.

Research methods

This article describes the results of ethnographical fieldwork based on semi-structured, face-to-face interviews performed in South Korea between 2006 and 2010.

We interviewed 18 persons, including a woman who had voluntarily donated her eggs for Hwang's research, as well as staff members of Korean WomenLink, an action group promoting gender equality. Another interviewee was a father who hoped that stem cell research would discover a treatment for his son's disability as soon as possible. We also interviewed the representatives of some non-profit organizations such as the Korean Organization for Rare Diseases. Others contacted are scholars in bioethics, medical doctors, journalists and a lawyer. Our interviews were mostly conducted in the Korean language. Hong is a native speaker of Korean and was usually the main interviewer, but we sometimes asked a Korean–Japanese translator for Tsuge and other non-Korean members in this research project.

In addition to our interviews, Hong participated in the seminars held by the Ministry of Health and Welfare in South Korea to discuss multiple issues about stem cell research, the meeting organized by the Korean Society of Bioethics to review the Hwang affair, and the workshop held by a women's network opposing egg donation for research purposes. Tsuge observed several Japanese government council meetings and the public hearing for stem cell research. Tsuge also participated in a seminar in Japan which included two journalists from a South Korean feminist newspaper (this was accessible on the Internet in 2006). We also held a public seminar inviting two activists from WomenLink in South Korea in 2007.

Altruism and patriotism

The report of the Korean National Bioethics Committee concluded that two researchers in Hwang's team had donated their eggs voluntarily rather than by compulsion. However, Hwang's power to influence the futures of the researchers in his team could not be ignored[1] (H. Hong 2008). Although we could not interview the two researchers in question, we would like to introduce a researcher, Dr K, by referring to archival documents. They reveal that Dr K's motivation for egg donation was to support treatment for sick children and her love for Korea.

Dr K was a PhD student in Hwang's team. She donated 19 eggs in 2003. According to her interview with *Nature* magazine, "she was happy to donate her eggs because she already had two children" (Cyranoski 2004b, p. 3). "In her original interview, she mentioned her desire to help sick children and her love for Korea" (Cyranoski 2004a, p. 14). However, she, along with Hwang, denied that his junior researchers' egg donations occurred (ibid., p. 13). Although she subsequently denied her egg donation, her donation became a big issue in May 2005. After Hwang's fabricated paper was revealed, Dr K reportedly resigned from her position. It was not only Dr K who was motivated to participate in egg donation to help sick children and to demonstrate love for Korea. More than 1000 women showed their willingness to donate their eggs for Hwang's research even after his data fraud was exposed. They also emphasized that their motivations for egg donation were to help sick children and to demonstrate their love for Korea.

Passion to help people: the case of Ms A

We met Ms A four times in 2006, 2007, 2009 and 2010. She was categorized as a voluntary egg donor in the report of the National Bioethics Committee. Since we tried to develop a rapport with Ms A, we did not record our interviews with her in 2006, 2007 and 2010. Thus, we recorded our interviews conducted in 2009 and partially in 2010 with her consent.

Right after the successful production of ES cells was published in *Science* magazine in 2004, Ms A read Hwang's book, *Naui seng-myong iyagi* (Hwang 2004), which means "Story of my life" in English. The book described Hwang's earnest effort to treat people with intractable disease and disability, which greatly moved Ms A since she had to take care of her uncle for a month after his liver transplantation. She wondered if Hwang's research could help people like her uncle. She was also impressed by people called "*arumdaun-saramdeul*," "beautiful people" in English,[2] a name granted to the voluntary egg donors in his book. He explained that "beautiful people" were the family members of patients with rare diseases, the ones involved in religious associations or women's associations. He continued as follows:

> It is said that the honour to the accomplishment in *Science* magazine is that of the women and that "Korean society has made the egg donors with pure and beautiful hearts who can release the pain of others". As in this case, each of the egg donors was labelled as the "beautiful people". (Hwang 2004, pp. 106–108)

Ms A soon excitedly called Hwang's office and met the professor in person. She immediately trusted him, which helped her to decide to donate her eggs in 2005. After her egg extraction, in contrast to the "little pain" mentioned in the book, Ms A had to be hospitalized and received treatment for ovarian hyper-stimulation syndrome (OHSS). After 29 eggs were extracted from her ovary, she was diagnosed with "moderate" OHSS at the hospital where her eggs had been retrieved.

When Ms A learned about Hwang being discredited, she felt helpless and could not talk about her experience of egg donation to anyone. She acutely lost weight and suffered from depression. She also had uterus inflammation. Eventually, she felt she had to give up her job. Although she strongly wanted to continue to trust Hwang after the initial report of his activities, she finally made the decision to convey her experience to a writer from a weekly magazine.

She explained her motivation for egg donation in our first interview. Her devout Christian family made her believe that she should help and love others. She said that she was obsessed by the idea that she could not help doing something when she saw anyone in trouble. Although she suffered from the adverse effects of egg retrieval, she believed she did good things by contributing to Hwang's research to bring new medical treatments. She added that she was disappointed by Hwang since he had deceived her and others and that she could no longer trust others.

When the women's group set up a hotline for "the victims of egg donation" for Hwang's research, Ms A contacted the group. Then the group offered Ms A financial support for her medical expenses. They also suggested that she should start a civil suit. After consideration, she decided to be a plaintiff with another woman also appealing for compensation. The reasons for claiming compensation were the following. First, the women were induced by deceptive information that the research was intended to treat ill people. They would not have donated their eggs if they had known that the research was actually far removed from clinical practice and that the two papers published in *Science* were fraudulent. Secondly, although they had signed informed consent forms about their egg donation, the forms did not contain accurate information about the adverse effects of the egg donation procedure. The women experienced more serious adverse effects than they had expected. They were not informed at all about the serious effects, such as the possibility of death. Ms A decided to publicize her experience because she wanted people to understand her true experience.

We also interviewed a lawyer, Ms B, twice, in 2007 and 2008. She was one of the counsel for the plaintiffs. The lawyer explained the plaintiffs' claims as above. In addition, the lawyer also pointed out the seriousness of the issue that only two among 119 women who had donated their eggs for Hwang's research had become plaintiffs and that all others had kept silent.

Just before our third interview with Ms A, she had lost the civil case in her first suit because the plaintiffs could not prove that their egg donation was relevant to their damaged health condition. Their signed consent forms also counted against them. Although Ms A was devastated after losing the case, she was still willing to appeal. Ms A had appealed after our third interview, but the other woman decided not to. Ms A lost her appeal in late 2009. When we asked why she had contacted the magazine to disclose her experience, she answered as follows:

> When reports about the fraud of the research result and the junior researchers' coerced egg donation were released, I realized my experience was not just my own problem. Although commercial egg donation and coerced egg donation were already recognized as problems, voluntary egg donation was not regarded as a problem. I thought I should bring to the attention of the public the issue of voluntary egg donation. I regret that I had donated without enough information about the adverse effects. At that time, egg donation for the research seemed something easy for me to do. In reality, I have suffered from terrible adverse effects. I hope that any women who consider egg donation positively and easily would learn the actual difficulties from my experience.

Ms A had decided to donate her eggs to Hwang's team because she was impressed by the kind action of "beautiful women," and she tried to emulate them. In the aftermath of the incident, she perceived herself as "a young, immature woman" when she had decided to donate her eggs. We also asked her what she felt about the title "saint woman" given to voluntary egg donors:

> At the beginning, I was bewildered by the reaction of the mass media which called me a saint woman because I donated my eggs for the sake of research. I had not expected

to be praised at all . . . Now I really get upset whenever I hear the term because I think the word represents people's typical definition of what women should be. They think that a woman who contributes her eggs to help others is a "saint." I am wondering then what they would call women who do not donate their eggs. To me, respecting egg donors is the same as demanding sacrifice from others, especially from women [in stem cell research].

After that time, she kept reconsidering the social meaning of her egg donation. With support from several women, mainly the members of the two women's groups acting for women's environments and gender equity, she also gradually changed her mind. However, she disclosed her mind to us in 2010 as follows:

I have been thinking about the identity of a "victim" through dance therapy and women's activities since last year. Feminists call me "a survivor" or "an experienced person" instead of "a victim" because the word includes gender discrimination. No word can express 100 percent of my present feeling. At least, I don't want to live as a "victim" anymore.

In her effort to re-find her identity, she seemed to swing between identifying with the traditional woman's virtue and the radical feminist's consciousness.

Hope for cure

In South Korea, the family bond is recognized as a strong tie (Leem and Park 2008). Parents and siblings tend to have a strong sense of responsibility in contributing to cure family members with incurable diseases or an abnormality. Non-compensated egg provision may be considered as a family member's role. In fact, according to the National Bioethics Committee, so-called voluntary donors said that their decision for donation was influenced by their acquaintance with patients and their families, members of the Korea Spinal Cord Injury Association, doctors in charge of patients, Hwang's team members, and members of the Association for Mothers with Sick Children (National Bioethics Committee 2006).

The profile of another woman who voluntarily donated her eggs to Hwang's research team was published in a paper. This woman later filed a lawsuit against the national government and the hospital because of her physical and psychological damage caused by egg retrieval under their sponsorship. This woman was advised to donate her eggs by her younger sibling who had suffered from an incurable disease. She was told at H. University Hospital that her eggs would be used for stem cell research tailored to individual patients. The hospital extracted her eggs in November 2004 (Son 2006a, pp. 6–7). She and her sibling were devastated when they heard of the fabrication of Hwang's paper. Thus, she also became a plaintiff with Ms A. After she lost her civil case, however, she did not appeal in the second suit, although she still suffered physically and psychologically from the adverse effects of her egg donation and Hwang's fabrication.

We also examined the significance of family values in the women's decisions to support Hwang's research for the people whose family members had serious illnesses or incurable abnormalities. We interviewed Mr C, a father who had a son with serious disability due to a traffic accident in 2008. He strongly supported Hwang's research and believed it would help his son recover. According to Mr C, when his son was hospitalized in order to cure his seriously injured nerve, a doctor introduced him Dr Hwang. His son was inordinately pleased because Dr Hwang promised to treat him. They deeply trusted Dr Hwang because of his generosity, and Mr C described his strong trust in Hwang:

> In South Korea, disabled people cannot be independent because of many factors such as insufficient social welfare and under-developed infrastructures. Disabled people cannot dream of having independent lives in South Korea. They hope to become able-bodied people. It is the biggest hope they have. You will understand that he [Dr Hwang] is a really good person if you see him. You can understand. I am confident. I have always trusted him [Dr Hwang]. All of my family members and relatives agree to support him.

As indicated in this interview, living with disability in South Korea is very difficult. In our interviews in 2008 with representatives of the Korean Organization for Rare Diseases, Mr C emphasized the difficulties in disabled people's lives and their hope for cure. He admitted his hope for cure brought by stem cell research in the near future and supported Hwang's study even after acknowledging the scandal. He also emphasized that family members would voluntarily donate their eggs for the research.

We should understand that disabled people, their families, and medical doctors place their hopes in the medical model. At the same time, we should realize that this is not just South Korea's situation. Around the world, many people with incurable diseases or disabilities strongly hope to be cured by stem cell therapy.

Discussion

Here, we discuss two ethical issues of "voluntary egg donation." First, we consider the emphasis on altruism involved in voluntary egg donation as an ethical issue. Second, we raise a question concerning compassion for those who suffer from incurable disease or disability. We consider that these two mentalities are strongly related to the ethical issues of voluntary egg donation though they are not usually realized as ethical problems.

The voluntary egg donors, called "beautiful people" in Hwang's book, symbolize Korean virtue, which precludes commercial egg donation. At the same time, the rush of women to donate their eggs for Hwang's stem cell research can be said to reflect a biopolitical order in which they voluntarily sacrificed their bodies for the national interest (Gottweis and Kim 2009, p. 233). It is unquestionably in the national interest to decline to accept financial gain from intellectual property rights involving science research. Furthermore, nationalism and the workings of a patriarchal society mobilized women as egg donors (Chekar and Kit-zinger 2007, Gottweis and Kim 2009). These points of view explain both women's implicit role as donors in the stem cell research (Dickenson 2006, Leem and Park 2008) and the commodification of women's bodies as egg suppliers (Son 2006b, Waldby 2008).

Even before the Bioethics and Safety Act was issued in 2005, the principle of anti-commercialism, such as the unpaid, voluntary egg donation, was an important ethical issue in South Korea. Nevertheless, it is well known that human eggs are already commodified in other countries, such as the US. Because of globalization, thousands of couples or single persons travel in order to acquire human eggs, sperm, and fertilized eggs. The American Society of Reproductive Medicine (ASRM) limits the amount of payment for the donation of gametes and embryos on the principle that monetary compensation of the donor should reflect only the time, inconvenience, and physical and emotional demands and risks associated with egg donation (ASRM 2008). However, an investigation in the US shows that many advertisements of egg donation agencies placed in over 300 college newspapers violate ASRM guidelines. It points out that almost one-quarter of advertisements offer payment in excess of $10,000 despite ASRM guidelines (Levine 2010). The National Academy of Sciences guideline stipulates the payment of only expenses, such as transportation costs, to egg donors (Kayukawa 2009). California State's law prohibits any compensation above the expenses involved in the donation. But as compensation alone does not attract egg donors, laws are violated. Finally, since 2009, the committee concerning stem cell research in New York State has started to allow payment of "compensation" up to $10,000 to women who supply their eggs for ES cell research (ibid.).

From a moral point of view, the analysis by Almeling pointed out that women are more likely to emphasize altruism in egg or sperm donation than men in the US. Almeling also points out that altruism expressed in nearly 100% of the egg donor profiles is derived from packaged representations, shaped by the donor's interests in being selected and the agency's interest in recruiting clients, and these interests are structured in part by gendered social norms (Almeling 2006, pp. 154–155). This view indicates the possibility that anti-commercialism requires women's altruism. Women's decisions to support medical research to help family members and others suffering from a grave disease are all too easily regarded as independent. An Ob/gyn we interviewed in 2007, Dr E, indicated a case in which there existed pressure among sisters to donate eggs for fertility treatment:

> I saw a case in which a mother took two of her daughters to our hospital and requested that we facilitate egg donation between the two women. I felt the mother was pressur-ing one of her daughters to donate her eggs to her sister. But it is not legal.

Yet many women in South Korea were always trying to understand their family members' feelings before they took their "voluntary" actions, and they indicated that "selfless love of their families" tended to be implicitly requested. Thus in reality, hidden factors affirm gender bias, and complicate the concept of choice in such a way that they require women to be material suppliers. This also happens in Japan. When one of us (Tsuge) participated in an open discussion about regenerative medicine in Japan in 2006, a representative of a parents' group of intractable disease patients stated that she would donate her eggs for research in regenerative medicine. Considering this type of cultural mentality in 2004, the Japanese Council of Science developed a policy regarding human eggs in the context of SCNT research into grave diseases. The policy states that voluntary offerings "should *not* be approved." Several council members feared that raising extravagant expectations among family members of patients with intractable diseases in the process of recruiting egg donors would put pressure on females to donate.

Another analysis of egg donation proceeds from the point of view of gender relations in South Korea. When we held a public seminar about the Hwang scandal in Japan in 2007, a speaker from Korean WomenLink mentioned the gender relationship in connection with compulsory military service for males. She showed that young men sometimes complained "why don't young women have to be conscripted?" Kwon demonstrates that compulsory male military service has played a crucial role in constructing the notions of citizenship, nationhood, masculinity, femininity, motherhood and fatherhood, creating the essential "glue" that binds each of these six potent ideas to the concept of the nation-state in contemporary South Korea (Kwon 2001). Kwon also suggests that the militaristic consciousness of women under the male conscription system affects women to such an extent that some adopt a self-sacrificial attitude. Although Kwon clearly stressed that not every man is drafted in reality, the gender logic behind conscription still affirms the notion of sacrificing young males.

It seems fair to say that women who feel sympathy for young males sacrificing themselves feel compelled to make their own sacrifice for the nation and/or other Koreans. This idea leads to another interpretation of voluntary egg donation. Korean women do not appear to be forced to donate their eggs; however, the gender roles in society push these female researchers to donate their eggs "voluntarily." In the case of women involved in egg donation for experimental scientific research, the women's compassion for sick or disabled persons was a compelling factor when added to the misleading information about the potential of their contribution to cure the sick. Our interview with Mr C, the father whose son was severely injured by an accident, helped us understand that families supporting their disabled members continued to expect new therapies from Hwang's research, and that they earnestly hoped to bring them back to normality. Furthermore, not only Ms A but also Dr K described their compassion for sick and disabled people as the motivation for egg donation, even after they knew the facts of Hwang's research. Anthropologist Scheper-Hughes considered the nature of gifting, family obligations, reciprocity and invisible sacrifice through her study on living donor transplant. On the basis of international data, she indicated a gender bias in living donation, with females as the more likely donors (Scheper-

Hughes 2007). She argues, "rather than celebrate the 'altruism' of women world-wide, we ought to be paying attention to the social pressures exerted on them to be living donors" (ibid., p. 508).

Moving to another contentious issue, we consider the economy of hope and healing behind the continuous drive to find cures for the disabled. The application of advanced technologies is sometimes presented as a catalyst to expand the choices of individuals. Opposition to the research drive for cures may be regarded as a violation of other people's freedom of choice, depriving them of a possible cure in future. On the other hand, opponents worry that the sick and the disabled might be labeled more distinctly than ever as people whose illness or disability should be treated (Tsuge 2002, Tremain 2006). This concern is similar to the problems identified by members of the disabled movement about emphasizing the importance of "cure." What they suffer is often mainly caused by social and cultural relationships, and an environment intolerant of disability. Unless this main cause is resolved, regenerative medicine may continuously accelerate the discrimination between the "normal" and the "abnormal," whatever hopes it could deliver.

Women living in society behave as subjects to voluntarily participate in science, while they are treated as objects of scientific experiment at the same time. Anyone who wishes to cure the discomfort and suffering of the disabled, and proactively participates in a scientific experiment, is at the same time treated as an object, in the quest to advance science to free society from disability, and increasingly from old-age diseases. We consider that such paradoxical surroundings induced the women in a roundabout way to donate their eggs for Hwang's research. We also take the lessons to heart that it could happen again anywhere in the world if we fail to understand the profound ethical issues around "voluntary" egg donation.

Acknowledgements

First of all, we are grateful to all interviewees for our research. Our research is a part of the research project "Medical Technologies and Gender" supported by Grant-in-Aid for Scientific Research (B) (No. 18310169) of the Japan Society for the Promotion of Science (JSPS) from April 2006 to March 2008. We would also extend appreciation to all members of the project, in particular Kaori Muto and Junji Kayukawa.

Notes

1. According to the yearbook of educational statistics in South Korea, the ratio of female faculty staff members in natural science and technologies in 2008 is 17.7%, and according to the investigation of scientific technology research developmental activity in 2007, the ratio of female scientists is 14.9%. (Ministry of Education and Technology 2010)
2. The meaning of "beauty" in Korean includes not only attractive appearance but also tender solicitude.

References

Almeling, R., 2006. Why do you want to be a donor? Gender and the production of altruism in egg and sperm donation. *New Genetics and Society*, 25 (2), 143–157.

ASRM (American Society for Reproductive Medicine), 2008. *Guidelines for gamete and embryo donation: a practice committee report* [online]. Available from: http://www.asrm.org/ Guidelines/ [Accessed 30 December 2010].

Chekar, C.K. and Kitzinger, J., 2007. Science, patriotism and discourses of nation and culture: reflections on the South Korean stem cell breakthroughs and scandals. *New Genetics and Society*, 26 (3), 289–307.

Cyranoski, D., 2004a. Crunch time for Korea's cloners. *Nature*, 429 (6987), 12–14.

Cyranoski, D., 2004b. Korea's stem-cell stars dogged by suspicion of ethical breach. *Nature*, 429 (6987), 3.

Dickenson, D.L., 2006. The lady vanishes: what's missing from the stem cell debate. *Bioethical Inquiry*, 3, 43–56.

Gottweis, H. and Kim, B., 2009. Bionationalism, stem cells, BSE, and Web 2.0 in South Korea: toward the reconfiguration of biopolitics. *New Genetics and Society*, 28 (3), 223–239.

Hong, H., 2008. What are problems in the egg donation for a research in the Hwang scandal? *In*: K. Tachi, ed. *Techno/bio politics*. Tokyo: Sakuhin-Sha, 196–214 [in Japanese].

Hong, S., 2008. The Hwang scandal that "shook the world of science." *East Asian Science and Society: An International Journal*, 2 (1), 1–7.

Hwang, W.-S., 2004. *Naui seng -myong iyagi* [Story of my life]. Seoul: Hyohyung-Chulpan [in Korean].

Hwang, W-S. *et al.*, 2004. Evidence of a pluripotent human embryonic stem cell line derived from a cloned blastocyst. *Science*, 303(5664), 1669–1640.

Hwang *et al.*, 2005. Patient-specific embryonic stem cells derived from human SCNT blastocysts. *Science* 308, 1777–1783.

Kayukawa, J., 2009. New York State allows payment for egg donor for science researches. *Medical Bio*, September, 81 [in Japanese].

Kwon, I., 2001. A feminist exploration of military conscription. *International Feminist Journal of Politics*, 3 (1), 26–54.

Leem, S. and Park, J., 2008. Rethinking women and their bodies in the age of biotechnology: feminist commentaries on the Hwang affair. *East Asian Science, Technology and Society: An International Journal*, 2 (1), 9–26.

Levine, A.D., 2010. Self-regulation, compensation, and the ethical recruitment of oocyte donors. *Hastings Center Report*, 40 (2), 25–36.

Ministry of Science and Education, 2010. Report on the statistics of women in science and technology 2009. Seoul, South Korea: Ministry of Science and Technology.

Myung, J., 2006. Embryonic stem cell research and women. *In: Proceedings of international forum: envisioning the human rights of women in the age of biotechnology and science*, 20–21 September 2006, Seoul. Seoul: Korean WomenLink, 191–202.

National Bioethics Committee, 2006. *Result of the survey of matter related to bioethics concerning egg donation process etc. of the Hwang's team*. Seoul: National Bioethics Committee, Ministry for Health and Welfare in South Korea.

Paik, Y., 2006. The traffic in eggs: Cultural constraction of ova 'donation' practice in Korea. Paper presented at the 2006 Annual Meeting of the Society for Social Studies of Science, 1–5 November 2006 Váncouver, Canada.

Scheper-Hughes, N., 2007. The tyranny of the gift: sacrificial violence in living donor transplants. *American Journal of Transplantation*, 7, 507–511.

Son, B., 2006a. The Hwang Woo-Suk case and the significance of a damage claim for victims of egg extraction. *WomenLink*, 4, 6–7.

Son, B., 2006b. Action against biotechnology: focused on activities of Korean WomenLink. *In: Proceedings of international forum: envisioning the human rights of women in the age of biotechnology and science*, 20–21 September 2006, Seoul. Seoul: Korean WomenLink, 102–110.

Tremain, S., 2006. Stemming the tide of normalization: an expanded feminist analysis of the ethics and social impact of embryonic stem cell research. *Biomedical Inquiry*, 3, 33–42.

Tsuge, A., 2002. Conflicts over new technology in genetic medicine. *In*: H. Hilgartner, Y. Nukaga and T. Ueyama, eds *Empirical bioethics in cultural context*, Proceedings of a workshop held jointly by Cornell University and Sophia University, 30 January to 1 February 2002, Sophia University, Tokyo. Tokyo: Sophia University Press, 91–104

Waldby, C., 2008. Oocytes markets: women's reproductive work in embryonic stem cell research. *New Genetics and Society*, 27 (1), 19–31.

Biological scarcity: looking beyond regulatory exteriors in Taiwan

Jennifer A. Liu

Department of Anthropology, University of Waterloo, Ontario, Canada

Research and bioethical policies are increasingly seen to facilitate, rather than to impede, scientific progress. Bioethical structures, nonetheless, often fail to account for or to shape the specific social surrounds in which scientific research is conducted. In Taiwan, a perceived shortage in human biological donations threatens to hamper stem cell research progress. This paper considers the stalled national biobank project and the lack of a reliable embryo supply for stem cell research, and suggests that one must look beyond regulatory structures in seeking explanations for such shortages. Specific aspects of Taiwan's democratization and social changes combine with problematic relations between patients and physicians to shape the terrain upon which human biologicals are given or withheld.

It wasn't like this in the UK. There the patients are more willing to donate their embryos for research because they have a good relationship between the public and the medical field. In Taiwan, I don't see this. I see the barriers to it and the distrust between levels of people. So it's difficult to use human embryos and to do this kind of research in Taiwan, because you probably can't get the number of embryos you need. (Dr Chen, interview, August 2006)

Dr Chen is a stem cell researcher at a prestigious Taiwanese laboratory.[1] He had returned home to Taiwan from the UK a few years earlier to participate in a national push to develop a strong biotech sector there. Whereas he had routinely used human embryos in his research in the UK, permissible under the established stem cell and embryo regulations there, he had yet to use a single one in Taiwan. In 2006, Dr Chen was actively working with many others to establish government policies regulating human embryo use and stem cell research in Taiwan. A year later, in 2007, he still had not used human embryos in his work even though official guidelines had been established. Part of Dr Chen's delay was due to a hesitation to work on human embryos in the absence of official permission to do so, but as he states above and repeated to me on other occasions, a lack of embryos is also a significant factor. In an informal survey that I conducted of 32 stem cell scientists, 69% stated that egg or embryo procurement was *the* major issue facing stem cell research in Taiwan.

Biomedical technoscience is unique in that it relies on public participation in a direct and bodily way. The national "Biomedtech Island" project seeks to establish Taiwan as an Asian hub for biotechnology and therapeutics, but such visions rely upon public acceptance and donation. Sheila Jasanoff argues that "democratic theory cannot be articulated in satisfactory terms today without looking in detail at the politics of science and technology" and that, furthermore, "the politics of biotechnology serves as a theater for observing democratic politics in motion" (2005, p. 6). Indeed, within the politics of science and technology, the participation of various publics has become a central aspect of scientific and governmental claims to legitimacy (Hayden 2003). Charis Thompson suggests that stem cell research emerges as a promising site in which to study global patterns of science and society, not only because of the ethical debates it has raised, but principally because stem cell research combines both research and medicine and represents the convergence of information technology, biotechnology, and business/finance (2010, p. 97). Similarly, Sarah Franklin, writing on stem cell research in the UK, calls stem cells a "global biological," and further suggests that through stem cell research, we can see how biological properties are increasingly created "in ways that reveal specific national and economic priorities, moral and civic values, and technoscientific institutional cultures" (2005, p. 61). And Aihwa Ong (2005) describes Singapore's push to build itself as an Asian biotech hub in which an initially imagined research environment unfettered by regulations is replaced by the development of a bioethical regime that is driven principally by an interest in developing a biotech economy.

Indeed, a bioethical regime in the form of policy documents, guidelines and regulations has become a necessary component of national biotech development, especially in relation to stem cell research involving human embryos. As Geoff Lomax, an important figure in California's stem cell policy development, has stated "regulations are not restrictions; they are enabling" (The Stem Cell Meeting, UCSF, 12–13 March 2007). Across the Pacific, Chen Zhu, then Vice-President of the Chinese Academy of Sciences, suggests that:

> Bioethics is not to hinder or fetter the advancement of science, but to create a good ethical environment to protect and promote the healthy development of science, and meanwhile impose necessary norms on it to urge it to defend human rights and dignity. (Chen 2006, p. 2)

Research regulation, in the form of bioethical policies, becomes an important aspect of research progress, especially in controversial practices of bioscience such as human embryonic stem cell research.

In Taiwan, stem cell research is viewed as significant in the nation's push to build itself as a major site of Asian biotech development. In 2005, after the famous South Korean Hwang Woo-Suk scandal, Taiwanese scientists, various scholars, and government officials redoubled their efforts to implement formal regulations governing human embryonic stem cell research (hESCR). A major force behind policy development was John Yu, head of Academia Sinica's stem cell program, and a member of the International Society for Stem Cell Research's (ISSCR) International Human Embryonic Stem Cell Guidelines Task Force. The resultant policies in Taiwan, "Policy Instructions on the Ethics of Human Embryo and Embryonic Stem Cell Research" were approved in 2007, and national legislation remains in review with the Executive Yuan branch of government. These documents specify the permissibility of the use and destruction of human embryos for research purposes with all of what have come to be viewed as relatively standard exceptions and conditions.

Despite the permissibility of using human embryos for research, now made explicit in the policy documents, human embryos are often difficult to obtain in Taiwan. Thus, while bioethical and regulatory structures provide an institutional framework within which to practice science, they often fail to consider or to shape the social arenas in which donations of requisite human biological materials take place. Rather, the social spaces of biological donation are shaped by multiple and often unpredictable influences. An unreliable embryo supply may seriously hamper stem cell research in Taiwan; limiting our vision to regulatory exteriors will shed little light on what is behind a perceived embryo shortage. Drawing on the case of the stalled national biobank project, I suggest that a scarcity of donation in Taiwan can be linked with particularities of Taiwan's democratization, including shifting relationships between experts and publics as well as a longer history of problematic physician–patient relationships. A reconfiguration is underway in which traditional relations – between expert and lay, between authority and subject – are shifting, and bioscientific research is called upon to use transparent practices of public consultation and other visible manifestations of deliberative democracy in order to enroll Taiwanese publics as research subjects and donors.

Methods

This paper draws on 14 months of ethnographic research conducted in Taiwan, mainly between 2005 and 2007. I traveled, attended meetings, and conducted interviews and observation throughout Taiwan, but most of my research was conducted in Taipei and Taoyuan counties in the north. Sarah Franklin and Celia Roberts describe ethnographic methods as:

> Whereby researchers immerse themselves in a range of different contexts to collect data about a particular object of inquiry, "following it around" to build up a kind of hyperstack of definitions, images, representations, testimonies, descriptions, and conversations. (2006, p. xix)

My "hyperstack" was built by following the discourses, people, and institutions involved in stem cell research and bioethics. Among others, I met with scientists, clinicians, lawyers, ethicists, philosophers, students, and religious leaders, and I attended numerous conferences, meetings, hearings, and talks. I attended weekly laboratory meetings and stem cell science classes at one research site, and I attended bioethics classes at another, all the while interviewing many people involved in stem cell science and policy making. Interviews were semi-structured and open-ended, and a handful of key informants were interviewed multiple times. I also read stacks of papers and made friends and talked with them about their ideas on various aspects of Taiwan's sciences, medical system, politics, identity, and everyday life.

Stem cell publics

Jasanoff proposes the concept of "civic epistemologies" as a way to denote cultural "collective knowledge-ways" with which societies adjudicate, make, test, deploy and accept or reject knowledge claims (2005, p. 255). As a kind of cultural form, civic epistemologies are relatively durable, but they can change under conditions of "shocks of exceptional severity" (Jasanoff 2005, p. 260). I suggest that Taiwan has undergone several such "shocks" including democratization.

Following 50 years of Japanese colonial rule (1895–1905), Taiwan was ruled by martial law until 1987 under the KMT Nationalist party, the longest period of martial law anywhere. After a period of reform and transition, full electoral democracy was established in 1996. Now, no longer subjects of colonial rule or martial law (though still claimed by China as a rebellious province), Taiwanese have realized themselves as free and freedom has become a significant narrative trope in everyday life (Liu 2008). For example, Dr Tao, a legal scholar exclaims, "The people have been emancipated!" Dr Tao played an important role in stem cell regulation and the biobank debates, and we were discussing public reactions to these projects. This was in July of 2007 when, amidst numerous accusations of corruption, calls for the resignation of then President Chen Shui Bian had escalated. Dr Tao captures the newfound sense of freedom that is coupled with shifting attitudes toward authority in Taiwan, exclaiming:

> Now there is no unchallengeable authority in Taiwan. Even the President! He is every day criticized and under fire! [laughs]. So you can imagine, it's hard for the scientists to claim so high an authority as before. (Dr Tao, interview, July 2007)

Dr Tao celebrates Taiwanese liberation from colonial, military, and authoritarian rule. Technocratic expertise, upon which Taiwan's "economic miracle" was built no longer confers unchallenged authority. Political and scientific authority, long entangled in Taiwan, are subject to increased scrutiny in a self-consciously democratic nation. These factors are illustrated in the tensions generated by the stalled national biobank project.

The Taiwan biobank

Von Kuei-Tien Chou (2007), analyzing Taiwan's Biomedtech Island project through the lens of risk society, suggests that technocrats and scientific elites have tended to monopolize the development of technological and industrial policy. Furthermore, they tend to model biotech projects on those of the successful IT sector. I have also heard this concern from stem cell researchers worrying about the relatively longer research time required for bioscientific production. In one case, a government grant for stem cell research provided funding for only two years, too short a period, they argued, to develop biotech applications. Chou suggests that this monopolization by technoscience elites, though it has previously had successful outcomes, lacks "democratic risk communication" and fosters tensions and "a serious widespread social distrust" (2007, p. 124, cf. Hollander and Mayo 1991, Irwin and Wynne 1996).

In the quotation at the beginning of this paper, Dr Chen attributes the differential embryo supplies in Taiwan and the UK to levels of social trust. Specifically, he refers to greater levels of social trust in the UK, and the quality of doctor–patient relationships more generally; in his narrative both serve to facilitate the "national embryo supply" in the UK (Franklin 2006). The distinction that Dr Chen makes between the respective embryo supplies in Taiwan and the UK is not reducible to one of East versus West. Indeed, Charis Thompson (2010) and Aihwa Ong (2010) show that in the other "Asian tigers" of Singapore and South Korea, egg and embryo donations are relatively common for stem cell research and are often framed as altruistic and patriotic acts.

The troubles encountered in the implementation of the Taiwan biobank help to illuminate the context in which an apparent reluctance to donate eggs and embryos occurs. As Asian countries advance in biomedical research, many projects are framed in terms of an ethno-biological specificity, in which projects of bio-science are geared toward regionally specific medical concerns. Aihwa Ong (2010) identifies the conjuncture between biocapitalism and biosecurity within imaginations and practices of Asian biotechnology in which a concern for the popu-lation is expressed in terms of both enhanced health and economics. The population is viewed as a resource for biological extraction and knowledge production as well as an object of ethical concern and therapeutic protection.

It is in this context and with these explicit concerns that the Taiwan biobank project was conceived. It is exemplary of the biocapital–biosecurity conjuncture that Ong identifies. The biobank was proposed as a way to create a valuable repo-sitory for both national science and therapeutics. To the surprise of its designers, however, the Taiwan biobank project has met with substantial social resistance. I suggest that the biobank project was conceptualized as a national resource with sig-nificant economic and therapeutic potential, but that a lack of understanding of emergent concerns and social change stymied its progress and has resulted in the production of a sphere of critical experts and reluctant publics. A combination of politically naïve scientific experts, an enhanced public engagement, a changing socio-political climate in which expertise is increasingly questioned, and an immature bioethical apparatus brought the biobank project to unanticipated controversy.

The biobank was designed to capitalize on Taiwan's existing strengths in IT and its national health insurance records. Bringing together existing data, blood samples and lifestyle information into a centralized state database, biobank promoters envisioned it as a way to improve population health while simultaneously promoting Taiwan's biotech development more generally. Minister Lin Feng-ching of the Science and Technology Advisory Group emphasizes the governmental rationale behind the biobank project and its role in international scientific competition more generally:

> We are building on our high-quality medical care facilities and the national health insurance program already in place ... With this series of programs, we can transform Taiwan into an important medical research center for genetic sciences in Asia ... We are under pressure of time to get the "Taiwan – Biomedtech Island" plan going as soon as possible. Both Singapore and China have also started on similar national biomedical databank projects in recent years ... We can compete well in the advanced biomedical fields and become the leader in the field in Asia. (*Taiwan Headlines 2005*)

The biobank is a project of the Institute of Biological Sciences at Academia Sinica, Taiwan's prestigious national research institution. A pilot study was scheduled to begin in May of 2005 with the goal of collecting 200,000 genetic samples from three areas of the island. This collection, it was thought, would provide an adequate sampling of Taiwan's major ethnic groups. Before the pilot study began, however, it met with significant resistance from Taiwan's "ELSI community" (ELSI is an acronym for ethical, legal and social implications and has become shorthand for a broad collection of social considerations that often exceed the named categories). In a talk a year later, an Academia Sinica scientist expressed his frustration with this ELSI community. Drawing on Taiwan's specific geography and genomes, its well-qualified scientific and medical experts, and its national health insurance system, he positions Taiwan as a unique and near-optimal site for assembling a national biobank. In addition, he notes a compliant research population as a specific strength in a slide stating, "Compliance of study participants: traditionally the compliance ... is very good. Traditionally the researcher ... acknowledges that to do a study in Taiwan is not difficult" (Dr Hsin, talk excerpt, May 2006).

Now, however, an ostensibly once compliant population resists, and Taiwan's strengths as a biobank site have been undermined by what Dr Hsin portrays as an overly zealous and under-informed ELSI community.

> The ELSI community in Taiwan has been very picky ... for example, initially the Taiwanese population was willing to let us use their health information, but currently we are criticized about whether we're using the health examinations to make the public

forget about informed consent or privacy or confidentiality. (Dr Hsin, talk excerpt, May 2006)

Dr Hsin later told me that the problem was that the ELSI people lack information. He recounted that he had spoken with them several times and had taught them a lot about the science, but now they returned as his interrogators for a project that is "easy to understand and ... very good for Taiwan." (personal communication)

Public understanding of science (PUS)

Many biobank scientists similarly express the need for greater public understanding of science (PUS). They emphasize the need for public education, transparency, and better communication with their publics. Two members of the biobank team explain that the project brings together scientific progress with a concern for the population. The biobank will "provide a huge resource for biomedical research" while also addressing common diseases in Taiwan, improving treatment and prevention, reducing medical costs, and making "it possible to achieve the goal of improving our nation's health" (Ou and Shen 2007, p. 3). They emphasize, "the most important thing is to communicate with the general public and to make them understand the importance of the Biobank and educate them in the development of science and genetic technology" (Ou and Shen 2007, p. 3). The underlying assumption evident in these narratives is that if the public were to understand the science then they would not have the current questions, concerns, or objections.

In her critique of the PUS model, Jasanoff elaborates how it assumes a deficit model of public understanding such that states can approach problems of public resistance to science through better dissemination of relevant information and education. In fact, Jasanoff argues, there exists little evidence that public ignorance of specific scientific facts meaningfully affects collective responses to technoscience. She further suggests that especially in the ways that PUS surveys are used in the US and Europe, PUS can be seen as "a kind of tacit democratic theory – a theory that presumes ignorant publics are in need of rescue by the state and grants science a privileged place in forming, and informing, an educated citizenry" (2005, p. 252). In Taiwan, I met several scholars, scientists, and public representatives who also resist the PUS narrative. They point instead to a lack of understanding on the part of the scientists. The society, and thus the research environment, they suggest, has changed.

> Before democratization the researchers, the scientists, were accorded very high social esteem, so they just did what they wanted to do as long as they didn't get involved in political controversies ... That said, times have changed. (ELSI scholar, interview, July 2007)

This scholar emphasizes that it is not simply public education that holds the answers to the controversies and questions raised by the biobank. Observations such as the one above suggest, rather, that the scientific community must itself become more aware of, and more sensitive to, the needs and concerns of a changing public sphere. It is a sphere in which scientific appeals and projects are not assumed to be self-justifying in the name of knowledge production, the nation, or the population. Rather, experts must be accountable to pluralistic and self-determining publics. A law professor involved in ELSI projects explains:

> They wanted to set up the biobank, and they took a traditional approach to their research. But that's the problem. They don't understand. Of course we cannot blame them a hundred percent, that's just the research way. They don't get their mistake. Because they don't get that the environment – or the public – has changed. The public wants to collect information about what the scientists are doing, and they don't trust the scientists a hundred percent. They have some concerns. And before they conduct their research, these concerns need to be clarified. (Dr Hsu, interview July 2007)

Where conventional models of the relationship between science and society tend to portray a fast moving realm of science with a social sphere lagging behind, Dr Hsu and others quoted above point to a fast changing society in which science "as usual" no longer functions. They invert conventional narratives that call for enhanced public understanding of science and call, instead, for a scientific community that takes seriously the task of understanding of its publics.

A nascent democratic consciousness flourishes within Taiwan's biotech. It requires that technocrats and scientific elites engage with other Taiwanese publics in a more equitable exchange of ideas and concerns, as well as benefits. Taiwan's specific political history of foreign occupation, martial law, democratization, and more recent divisive politics and corruption scandals all serve to undermine Taiwanese publics' trust and confidence in their leaders – political and scientific. In a climate of enhanced attention to democratic representation and self-determination, citizens are becoming increasingly concerned about the uses to which their biological information and samples are subject. Thus, what began as an ostensibly straightforward exercise in collecting blood samples from Taiwan's multiple ethnic groups in the interest of creating a national biobank has become an exercise, instead, in public controversy. Terence Hua Tai and Wen-Tsong Chiou point to societal changes and shifts in public attitudes in relation to the biobank project:

> During the last decade, Taiwan has been undergoing a rapid process of democratization, and nowadays a strong conviction can easily be detected in public discourse that such basic values in a pluralistic democratic society as personal autonomy and social justice should be accorded moral weight to be balanced against the familiar appeal to national prosperity or general welfare. (Tai and Chiou 2008, pp. 105–106)

As Tai and Chiou articulate, a societal shift toward enhanced valorization of democratic principles and individualism shapes the ground upon which national science is now practiced. Mark Moskowitz further attributes "the birth of an age in which self orientation (*ziwo, zijue*) came to represent liberation rather than selfishness for the first time in Taiwan's history" (2008, pp. 328–329) to the rapid economic leap of the mid-1980s. These shifting attitudes are reflected in broadening discussions regarding human rights, self-determination, and social justice and are specifically visible in a host of social concerns expressed in relation to the biobank project.

Patient–doctor relations

Physicians serve an important role in the procurement of human embryos for stem cell research. As Thompson (2010) suggests, stem cell research occupies the spectrum from basic scientific bench research to bedside therapeutics. Embryo procurement often relies on a movement from bedside to bench as most embryos come from procedures involved with in vitro fertilization. As the biobank project shows, individuals and groups in Taiwan are increasingly questioning the ways in which their biological samples and donations will be used, and are challenging scientific expertise. The problems faced by the organizers of the biobank, and by stem cell researchers waiting for embryos, take place in a social arena in which expertise and authority more generally are called into question.

In this context, the relationship between patients and their doctors is increasingly both important and problematic. Accounts of deteriorating patient–doctor relationships abound in the media and were a recurring theme in my interviews. However, tensions within doctor–patient relationships have a longer history in Taiwan. Ming-Cheng Lo (2002) shows that during the Japanese colonial period this relationship was strained when doctors refused to reduce their fees in the midst of an economic downturn. Arthur Kleinman (1995) has shown how physicians in Taiwan in the 1960s and 1970s occupied ambivalent social roles, viewed at times as greedy and even dangerous. And Holliday and Tam remind us that in Japan, South Korea and Taiwan, "healthcare was initially left chiefly to the market (2004, p. 762).

At present, public views on doctors appear to be worsening. A PhD student in stem cell biology sits at his lab bench and emphasizes that it is sometimes difficult to do human research in Taiwan. Embryos, for instance, can be in scarce supply. He explains that researchers and physicians need to work to build better relationships if they expect to gain public support for their work. He explains, "the relationship between physicians and patients is often not one of cooperation in Taiwan," which he demonstrates by making two fists and pressing them hard against each other. He continues, "the physicians ask permission and they have the patients sign a paper, but it's not clear and it doesn't often communicate what it has to do with the patients" (interview, March 2006). Here, he suggests that consent forms represent a clinician's interest in obtaining written consent rather than in confirming that a patient has a full understanding of the stakes and risks. This kind of instrumentalism within the patient–doctor relationship undermines the establishment of a more durable trust.

A senior stem cell researcher, who is active in policy development, similarly attributes the difficulty in obtaining human research embryos to the deteriorating doctor–patient relationship:

> I don't know why we have this problem. Maybe it's because of our cultural background or maybe because the physicians in Taiwan didn't do things in the proper way, so they lost the trust of the public. And then this creates a bad emotional cycle because the patients don't trust them, and so then the doctors, maybe they don't tell the patient and then just do some things anyway. (Interview, August 2006)

These stem cell scientists emphasize a loss of trust based on a range of reasons from poor communication to deliberate physician malfeasance. Recognizing the role of scandal, journalist Laura Li also succinctly captures some of the central dynamics of the deteriorating physician–patient relationship, locating it in the move within medicine from a focus on relationality and healing to a market orientation.

> Repeated scandals, from incorrect medication and falsification of medical records, to an injured child being refused emergency treatment, are making medicine a high-risk profession full of pitfalls for practitioners, and are rapidly eroding health-care personnel's status in society.

> Medicine has traditionally been a vocation, a calling to heal and save. But today doctors and patients seem to stand at opposite ends of a market transaction. (Li 2005, p. 3)

Although the market component within medicine is not new in Taiwan, health-care transactions take place in a changed social context. Exacerbating these tensions, many stories of scandal involve accounts of illicit biological sampling of Taiwan's Aborigines. The Aborigines have been identified within population genetics as "isolates" of historical and scientific interest (Reardon 2005) and portrayed as among the most genetically homogeneous populations in the world (Lin *et al.* 2000). Viewed thus as important genetic repositories, stories circulate about Aboriginal blood samples being collected without adequate informed consent; these include numerous accounts of blood taking for research disguised as free health checks, and other accounts of surreptitious collecting. As international concern for the rights of indigenous peoples mounts, and as Aborigines in Taiwan become increasingly visible as specific subjects of political and social concern, stories of improper scientific collecting, patenting, and commodification serve to further undermine the credibility of doctors in Taiwan.

The aforementioned insights from stem cell researchers and a journalist point to the constitutive role of trust in obtaining biologicals for research and within circulations of genetic materials more broadly (Sleeboom-Faulkner 2008). Steven Epstein (2007) also shows the role that collective memories play in shaping trust in relation to projects of medicine and science. As Taiwan's publics begin to demand more accountability from their political, scientific and medical authorities more generally, stories of medical malfeasance continue to emerge, which further undermines patients' trust.

Conclusion

Years of work that includes multi-stakeholder meetings, public surveys, consultations with religious leaders, and ongoing debates about how best to regulate stem cell research and human embryo use in Taiwan resulted in the development and adoption of formal guidelines. Yet, despite adherence to international standards and protocols, the lack of a reliable embryo supply threatens to hamper Taiwan's competitiveness in stem cell research.

Taiwanese publics are not historically reluctant to donate their biological materials. For instance, the Buddhist Tzu-Chi Bone Marrow Registry, established in 1993, became by 1998 the largest bone marrow registry in Asia (Shaw *et al.* 1999). And as mentioned previously, researchers previously regarded Taiwanese as compliant study subjects. But whereas the Tzu-Chi registry was promoted as a charitable and humanitarian project, the value orientations of current biomedical research are more market oriented. As Liu and Tai (2008) suggest, benefit sharing may need to be built into projects such as the biobank that rely upon biological donations (cf. Hayden 2007). And Laura Li and others show how doctor–patient relations are increasingly conceptualized in transactional market terms.

Drawing upon experiences from the stalled national biobank project in Taiwan, I suggest that a multiplicity of factors is implicated in Taiwanese publics' emergent reluctance to donate to biological research. Importantly, these factors are shaped within the context of a radically democratic consciousness that founds a more skeptical attitude toward both political and scientific authority and creates a demand for a new relationship between experts and publics, as is demonstrated in tensions in patient–doctor relationships more broadly.

The establishment of an intact bioethical regime appears to be a necessary component of modern biotech. As Geoff Lomax and Chen Zhu clearly state, and as national bioethical developments suggest, regulations facilitate biotech research. However, a focus on regulatory exteriors can obscure, as this volume shows, actual practices and relationships on the ground in Asia. Bioethical regulations, and tensions, are shaped in an increasingly international arena; this is especially true for stem cell research and biobanks. Dr Hsin, the frustrated biobank scientist mentioned earlier, told me that they had no problems with the research project until they started calling it a biobank. This underlines the transnational nature of bioethical discourses and networks that shape the emergence of what counts as a bioethical problem. This transnational character, in turn, suggests that it is through the development of bioethical regulatory measures that conform to international standards that a first level of response to issues of bio-scarcity may be addressed. The case of Taiwan suggests, however, that this is, indeed, only a first level and minimal response and that serious attention to broader social concerns and public consultations will be required if publics are to be enrolled bodily in biological projects.

Acknowledgements

The research and writing of this article was supported by fellowships from the Freeman Foundation, the Fulbright Foundation, the California institute for Regenerative Medicine, the Charlotte W. Newcombe Foundation, the Townsend Center for Humanities and UC Berkeley's Science and Technology Studies Center. I am greatful to Margaret Sleeboom-Faulkner for her energetic and generous support, and to the anonymous reviewes for their rich feedback.

Note

1. All names given for quoted excerpts are pseudonyms as required by my IRB and anthropological protocol.

References

Chen, Z., 2006. Unity but not uniformity: globality and locality of bioethics, *Paper presented at the 8th World Congress of Bioethics*, 6–9 August, Beijing.

Chou, V.K.T., 2007. Biomedtech Island project and risk governance: paradigm conflicts within a hidden and delayed high-tech risk society. *Soziale Welt*, 58, 123–143.

Epstein, S., 2007. *Inclusion: the politics of difference in medical research*. Chicago: University of Chicago Press.

Franklin, S., 2003. Ethical biocapital: new strategies of cell culture. *In*: S. Franklin and M. Lock, eds. *Remaking life and death: toward an anthropology of the biosciences*. Santa Fe: School of American Research Press, 97–128.

Franklin, S., 2005. Stem Cells R Us: emergent life forms and the global biological. *In*: A. Ong and S. Collier, eds. *Global assemblages: technology, politics, and ethics as anthropological problems*. Malden, MA: Blackwell, 59–78.

Franklin, S., 2006. From the cyborg embryo to transbiology: the IVF–stem cell interface in the UK, Invited lecture, 15 November, UC Berkeley.

Franklin, S. and Roberts, C., 2006. *Born and made: an ethnography of preimplantation genetic diagnosis*. Princeton, NJ: Princeton University Press.

Hayden, C., 2003. *When nature goes public: the making and unmaking of bioprospecting in Mexico*. Princeton, NJ: Princeton University Press.

Hayden, C., 2007. Taking as giving: bioscience, exchange, and the politics of benefit-sharing. *Social Studies of Science*, 37 (5), 729–758.

Holliday, I. and Tam, W. K., 2004. E-health in the East Asian Tigers. *International Journal of Medical Informatics*, 73, 759–769.

Hollander, R. and Mayo, D., eds., 1991. *Acceptable evidence: science and values in hazard management*. New York: Oxford University Press.

Irwin, A. and Wynne, B., eds., 1996. *Misunderstanding science? The public reconstruction of science and technology*. Cambridge: Cambridge University Press.

Jasanoff, S., 2005. *Designs on nature: science and democracy in Europe and the United States*. Princeton, NJ: Princeton University Press.

Kleinman, A., 1995. Anthropology of bioethics. *In*: A. Kleinman, ed. *Writing at the margin: discourse between anthropology and medicine*. Berkeley: University of California Press, 41–67.

Li, L., 2005. Editor's note. Translated by R. Taylor. *Sinorama*, 30(5), 3.

Lin, M., *et al.*, 2000. Heterogeneity of Taiwan's indigenous population: possible relation to prehistoric Mongoloid dispersals. *Tissue Antigens*, 55, 1–9.

Liu, H.E. and Tai, T.H., 2008. Public trust, commercialization, and benefit sharing: towards a trustworthy biobank in Taiwan. *In*: M. Sleeboom-Faulkner, ed. *Human genetic biobanks in Asia: politics of trust and scientific advancement*. London: Routledge, 27–39.

Liu, J.A., 2008. *Biomedtech nation: Taiwan, ethics, stem cells and other biologicals*, Thesis (PhD). University of California San Francisco and Berkeley.

Lo, M.C., 2002. *Doctors within borders: profession, ethnicity, and modernity in colonial Taiwan.* Berkeley: University of California Press.

Moskowitz, M., 2008. Multiple virginity and other contested realities in Taipei's foreign club culture. *Sexualities*, 11 (3), 327–351.

Ong, A., 2005. Ecologies of expertise: assembling flows, managing citizenship. *In*: A. Ong and S. Collier, eds. *Global assemblages: technology, politics, and ethics as anthropological problems*. Malden, MA: Blackwell, 337–353.

Ong, A., 2010. Introduction: an analytics of biotechnology and ethics at multiple scales. *In*: N. Ong and N. Chen, eds. *Asian biotech: ethics and communities of fate*. Durham, NC: Duke University Press, 1–51.

Ou, C.H. and Shen, C.Y., 2007. The Taiwan biobank project: for the health of future generation [online]. *Academia Sinica E-news*, 12, 19 April [online]. Available from: http://newsletter. sinica.edu.tw/en/letter [Accessed 6 January 2008].

Reardon, J., 2005. *Race to the finish: identity and governance in an age of genomics*. Princeton, NJ: Princeton University Press.

Shaw, C.K., *et al.*, 1999. Marrow donor registry and bone marrow transplantation from unrelated donors in Taiwan: initial experience of the Tzu Chi Taiwan Marrow Donor Registry (TCTMDR). *Bone Marrow Transplantation*, 23, 727–730.

Sleeboom-Faulkner, M., 2008. *Human genetic biobanks in Asia: politics of trust and scientific advancement*. London: Routledge.

Tai, T.H. and Chiou, W.T., 2008. Equality and community in public deliberations: genetic democracy in Taiwan. *In*: V. Launis and J. Räikkä, eds. *Genetic democracy*. New York: Springer, 105–120.

Taiwan Department of Health Executive Yuan, Bureau of Medical Affairs, 2007. Policy Instructions on the Ethics of Human Embryo and Embryonic Stem Cell Research [online]. Available from:// www.tsscr.org.tw/en_ver/guide_02.htm [Accessed 12 December 2007].

Taiwan Headlines, 2005. Government launches plan to setup R&D health centers, Taiwan Headlines [online]. Available from: http://English.www.gov.tw//TaiwanHeadlines/index.jsp?categid+10& recorded=81679 [Accessed 25 January 2006]

Thompson, C., 2010. Asian regeneration? Nationalism and internationalism in stem cell research in South Korea and Singapore. *In*: A. Ong and N. Chen, eds. *Asian biotech: ethics and communities of fate*. Durham, NC: Duke University Press, 95–117.

Overcoming embryonic exceptionalism? Lessons from analyzing human stem cell research regulation in Israel

Barbara Prainsack

School of Social Science & Public Policy, King's College London, London, UK

This paper discusses the role of religious and Zionist endorsements of scientific and technological progress in preparing the ground for a permissive regulation of human embryonic stem cell research in Israel. I argue that the Israeli case demonstrates that science does not mean anything at an abstract level but it only means something as science for a particular goal, or in a particular context. Moreover, it suggests that taking discussions about the moral status of embryos as starting points for comparative analyses of regulatory approaches towards embryonic stem cell research limits the scope and fruitfulness of the investigation as it "locks" our gaze in a particular direction. I conclude by arguing that considering how certain regulatory responses became *necessary*, rather than merely *possible*, in a given societal and political context, can further sharpen our analysis.

Introduction: a necessary leader? Human embryonic stem cell research in Israel

Israel is a "powerhouse" in human embryonic stem cell (hESC) research, an article in *The Jerusalem Post* announced in 2006. In terms of numbers of publications in scientific journals, Israel ranked second just after the US: "way ahead of the UK, Korea, China, Singapore, Australia, Sweden and Canada" (Siegel-Itzkovich 2006). Despite its position at the forefront of hESC research worldwide (Margulies 2006, Stafford 2006, Simonstein 2008), Israel has no explicit legislation or regulation pertaining to hESC specifically. The derivation and cultivation of stem cells from human embryos is guided by the regulatory framework pertaining to the experimentation with human materials. Proposals for research involving hESC must be approved by the Helsinki Committee for Genetic Medical Experiments on Humans (see also Barilan and Siegal 2005). In 2001, a recommendation by the Bioethics Advisory Committee of the Israeli Academy of Sciences and Humanities (IASH) endorsed the use of embryos which were created for IVF purposes but are no longer needed for that purpose, as well as embryos created through somatic cell nuclear transfer ("cloned" embryos) as sources for hESC research. However, the Committee did not condone the use of embryos created for research purposes via gamete fusion (IASH 2001). The reason for this is a religious one: according to Jewish Law (*Halacha*), men are not allowed to perform *hash-hatat zera*, the "improper emission of seed," that is, they may not engage in any activity in which sperm would be "destroyed" without having had the chance to contribute to procreation (see Feldman 1968).

As this latter example illustrates, despite the fact that the Committee comprised a range of religious and non-religious experts, these recommendations are in line with religious Jewish Law. Jewish Law does not allow the creation of embryos for research purposes due to the aforementioned prohibition on using sperm for any other than reproduction purposes; but it does not object to the use of "surplus" IVF embryos as *ex utero* embryos do not have any independent human dignity (Lavi 2008, Eidelman and Halperin 2009). Although the IASH Bioethics Advisory Committee's recommendations are not legally binding, they correspond with actual practices in the field. This is the case because of the highly influential nature of Jewish Law in Israeli society and policy making, despite the fact that the majority of Israel's population is comprised of groups which are either not strictly religious or not even Jewish. This particularity of the role of religious law in Israel has been discussed in the literature (e.g. Gross and Ravitsky 2003), and it accounts for relatively uniform practices and moral assessments regarding what is permissible to do in the field of embryo research and what is not.

The primary sources of ES cells in Israel are embryos left over from IVF treatments (Simonstein 2008, p. 732). Compared with other countries, spare embryos are readily available, because of the widespread and intense use of assisted reproduction techniques in the country (see Birenbaum-Carmeli and Carmeli 2010).[1] Women or couples with frozen embryos left over from IVF treatments are asked at regular intervals whether they want to keep them in storage, to donate them to other women or couples, to donate them to research, or to have them destroyed (Barilan and Siegal 2005).

In the following section I will argue that in addition to Jewish teachings pertaining to research on human embryos, which provide fewer barriers to human embryonic stem cell (hESC) research than is the case in predominantly Christian regions of Europe and North America, Jewish religion and traditions also contain a generally positive attitude to science and technology which contribute to providing a fertile ground for stem cell research. Thus, a strong positive emphasis on science and technology is present in religious teachings, Zionist traditions and values, and in current political discourses. In consequence, many segments of society are exposed if not to an explicit imperative to support scientific and technological progress, then at least to narratives that value them positively (to the extent that they do not conflict with other Jewish values).

The positive attitude towards the value and function of science and technology challenges assumptions which are still held by some stakeholders at the interface of science and society, namely that scientific experts are more supportive of science than "lay" publics, and that the more knowledgeable people are about science, the more supportive they tend to be.[2] In many instances in Israeli policy making, orthodox religious leaders, not scientists, were the most emphatic supporters of per-missive science regulations, because science was seen as an enabling factor for many religious objectives (procreation, fostering health, etc.). Thus the Israeli case illustrates that the term "science" in public understanding of science is never really without a preposition: science is always science *for* a particular purpose, or science *in* a particular context. Furthermore, the Israeli case suggests that the common tradition of what I suggest calling "embryonic exceptionalism" in explaining resistance to or support for hESC research is limited in its fruitfulness. The practice of assessing national differences in regulatory approaches towards, and discourses on, hESC research primarily through the lens of the status of the embryo has blurred our view for the notion that embryos are not stable entities: they receive meaning through the ways we engage with their future forms and manifestations (see also the notion of "relational ethics" used by Hashiloni-Dolev and Weiner 2008). I conclude by arguing that examining policies in the field of hESC research as necessary answers to questions of vital political currency can be instructive in understanding differences in regulatory approaches across nations.

This paper draws upon a re-evaluation of the material I gathered while doing fieldwork in Israel on several occasions between December 2001 and August 2003. The material consisted of data from interviews with policymakers, ethicists, and scientists, and notes from informal conversations with professional experts and "lay" people. First findings from this study were published in 2005 and 2006 (Prainsack and Firestine 2005, 2006, Prainsack 2006). For this paper, I went back to my field notes, earlier drafts of my PhD thesis (University of Vienna, 2004), and I also considered feedback that I had received on several occasions when presenting my work in Israel.

Trusting science

In contrast to the assumption that differences in religious teachings and values are the most important factors explaining regulatory approaches to stem cell research across nations (on the overlap between religious and "secular" arguments, see Myskja 2009), several narratives complement and mutually enhance each other in creating an exceptionally permissive atmosphere for hESC research in Israel (Prainsack 2006). First of all, religious values indeed play an important role in shaping positive attitudes towards hESC, both in rendering this field of research morally unproblematic, and also by framing every research activity as a potentially important activity in the quest for creating and improving life. But religious narra-tives cannot explain why support for hESC can be found in virtually every segment of the political spectrum in Israel, religious and secular alike. This can only be understood if we also take into consideration the political discourse revolving around demographics, which provides a frame (Goffman 1974, Schön and Rein 1994) of "risk" to discussions of scientific advance: the collective body of the Jewish Israeli population is perceived as being in danger (Prainsack 2006). When I carried out fieldwork in Israel, many so-called "hawks" felt that more Jewish babies were needed because "[t]he womb of the Arab woman," as Arafat had once stated, was his "strongest weapon" (cf. Foa 2002; see also Kanaaneh 2002). Some "doves" felt that given that Israel, according to the Declaration of Independence (1948), is both a Jewish state and a democracy, it is important to maintain a Jewish majority in order not to lose the legitimacy to retain Jewish values and "be safe" in the Middle East. Also the risk of being killed in a war or in a terrorist attack seemed to have an impact on the value attached to procreation: as one of my informants put it, one child is never enough because he or she could die in a war. Some also mentioned that it was the duty of post-Holocaust generations to try to help "compensate" (in numerical terms) for the loss of Jewish lives in the *Shoah*.

But it is the widespread high level of trust in science and technology that prepares the ground for the collective embrace of hESC research in Israel. The important position which scientific and technological advance assumes in public and political life in Israel is intimately linked to the heritage of Zionism (Prainsack and Firestine 2005, 2006). In the Zionist movement, technical expertise has served two goals at the same time: it has made possible, at a technical and logistical level, the mass immigration to the area during British Mandate, and it "epitomized the secular knowledge that many Zionists felt would existentially transform Jews into a people like the nations of the world" (Penslar 1991, p. 7). Thus, science and technology were not only seen as enabling the Jewish existence in the Middle East, but they were also destined to serve as common denominators for all Jews, whether religious or secular, European or oriental. Indeed, science and technology soon assumed the role of a "civil religion"[3] (to borrow Meira Weiss' term; see Weiss 2002, p. 6) in the country.

However trust in science and technology has not only shaped Israeli science and technology regulation via the "detour" of Zionism, but it is rooted in Jewish teachings and traditions itself. The Zionist influence in Israeli state and society has stabilized rather than generated the high esteem in which scientific and technological advance is held in wide sectors of the society. Noah J. Efron (2007), in his book *Judaism and science*, reminds us of the particular role that nature plays in the Jewish Bible. According to Mircea Eliade (1959), Salo Baron (1952), and others, the beginning of Judaism represents a break with natural religions and the beginning of an importance of historical memory. In the words of G. Ernest Wright (1950, pp. 19–20; cf. Efron 2007, p. 33), the God of the Israelites was "no immanent power in nature nor in the natural process of being and becoming. The nature of his being and will is revealed in historical acts." Thus, "Jewish religion has been from the very beginning [...]

an *historical* religion, in permanent contrast to all *natural* religions" (Baron 1952, pp. 1, 4, cf. Efron 2007, p. 33). Similarly, Umberto Cassuto (1961) argues that because God was seen as exempt from, and above, nature, a "dispassion" (Efron 2007, p. 33) towards nature was evident among biblical Jews (for a critical discussion see Leavitt 1998).

This "dispassionate" attitude towards nature is still prevalent in many Jewish Israeli communities. This, however, does not mean that people are indifferent towards pollution, or the destruction of nature, for example. Instead, nature is related to in a utilitarian manner: it is valued where it serves human health and wellbeing, and where it assists humans in fulfilling God's commandments. The positive meaning attached to nature is always mediated by another good that nature serves, or is destined to serve, in the realm of human life. In Efron's (2007, p. 62) words, "natural knowledge was embraced in direct proportion to its usefulness." Against this backdrop it seems plausible that scientific and technological advances which help to improve nature (our natural environment, our food, our bodies) are not perceived as standing in contrast, or posing a threat, to nature. By helping to tame, control, manipulate and "enhance" nature, science and technology assume a role which is entirely compatible with religious conceptions of hierarchy and order. It is probably no coincidence that many Jewish religious authorities enthusiastically accepted Darwin's theories from the start (Efron 2007, pp. 178 and 202).

The high value attached to science and technology is not merely an additional feature which Zionism added to longstanding Jewish traditions. Instead, Zionism transposed inherently Jewish values and imperatives into a secular vernacular. Today, it is a core building block of the country; as mentioned before, it did not only enable the establishment of the state (by providing the means to "tame" nature and render the desert inhabitable), but in the form of military technology and reproductive technology it has since assumed the role of protecting the continuity of the Jewish state in the Middle East. The link between military and reproductive technologies, by the way, is more explicit than one might assume: as Susan Martha Kahn (2000) and Meira Weiss (2002) have illustrated, women are sometimes explicitly portrayed as soldiers serving their country by bearing children. But even in instances in which this link is less apparent, military and reproductive technologies have something in common: they both have a particular concern for life at their core: a concern about the quality and the quantity of life in the Jewish state.

In sum, the positive attitude towards hESC research in Israel is not merely the result of the absence of religious prohibitions pertaining to embryo research, but it is rendered *necessary* by a risk discourse revolving around the continuity of the Jewish state, and the Jewish collective, in the Middle East. Public discussions about Jewish vs. Arab and/or Muslim demographics represent a problem in need of a solution. It is due to the high trust in science and technology, which is grounded both in Jewish religion and traditions and in Zionism, that the answer to this problem is primarily phrased in scientific and technological terms. It is military and medical scientific/technological advance which is seen to protect the Jewish collective in Israel and guarantee its survival. This solution works because despite the fact that no political consensus can be achieved on political solutions to the crisis in Israel (whoever is seen as the main population at risk, "Palestinians," "settlers," Arab Israelis, secular Jews, etc.), the virtually universal embrace of science and technology bridges political, "ethnic" and partly also religious gaps and provides a common language for problem solution. It is also for this reason that it is inconceivable (Prainsack 2006) that anybody would challenge scientific or technological solutions. Those who do challenge them nevertheless find themselves outside the spectrum of the "thinkable and sayable," with the result that they are labeled as "irrational" or "strange." One actor's resistance to accepting opposing opinions as legitimate and potentially equally reasonable viewpoints went as far as questioning the sanity of a person who presented the argument: when confronted with the claim of (then) chairman of the US President Bush's Council on Bioethics, Leon Kass, that human beings had some kind of natural instinct to reject genetic manipulation, one bioethicist whom I interviewed in Israel said that Kass had "a psychological problem" (cf. Prainsack and Firestine 2005, p. 361).

The meaning of Israeli embryos

Science for a purpose

Trust in science and technology, grounded in Jewish religion, and imprinted in Israel's state institutions and society via its endorsement by Zionism, is prevalent in all sectors of Israeli society. As mentioned above, on numerous occasions of science policy making in Israel, the most fervent supporters of medical and technological advance, and permissive regulation, were religious individuals, not scientists. Similarly, religious sectors of society have not been found to be more skeptical of technological advance[4] than secular sub-populations, as is the case in Christian countries (see, for example, Gill 2005, Jones 2005, Engelhardt 2007, Prainsack et al. 2007). This insight does not only challenge the last remaining bastions of those believing in the deficit model – the idea that public skepticism of science is due to insufficient knowledge, and that overcoming this knowledge "deficit" leads to more public support. It also questions the conception of "public understanding of science" as a concept where "science" means anything at an abstract, de-contextualized level. Science and technology only mean something in so far as they are understood as science and technology for a certain purpose, and in a certain context. Jewish Israeli publics are supportive of science and technology because, and in so far as, they have been perceived to be facilitators for the collective Jewish Israeli existence in the Middle East.

Overcoming embryonic exceptionalism?

Insights obtained from the Israeli case study have a clear implication for research into rationales underlying the governance and regulation of stem cell research in other countries. First, permissive or restrictive policies towards hESC research should not be over-explained by referring to religious "values." A search in any database of scholarly resources shows that the academic literature in this field revolves around religious perspectives and religious values, although it is never such abstract values that inform policy making. Instead, it is the ways in which such values are mobilized to give answers to larger societal, political or historical questions that govern regulatory approaches. The scope of these questions can be very broad; they are not limited to embryo research, and not even to medical research more generally (see, for example, Green 2008). In Jewish Israeli societies, science and technology are mobilized to solve problems of military security in a manner very similar to the way in which they are employed to potentially cure diseases, alleviate infertility, and increase the number of healthy babies (for example, both receive considerable support and public resources, and they are sometimes justified with the same arguments). Thus, an implication from the Israeli case is that we may not be able to fruitfully continue to employ embryonic exceptionalism, namely the assumption that debates about the moral status of the embryo structure all discursive space in this field, and that such debates are therefore the first place to turn to when we try to understand and explain different regulatory approaches towards hESC research. Ingrid Metzler (2007) in her study on hESC in Italy, for example, argues that embryos as such do not have any independent meaning at all; they obtain meaning by the way in which they are embedded in discourses on family relations, religious teleologies, or therapeutic expectations (see also Geesink *et al.* 2008, Hashiloni-Dolev and Weiner 2008, Prainsack *et al.* 2008).

Possibilities and necessities

Furthermore, while much academic work looking at discourses in the field of research regulation revolves around conditions which render a particular regulatory framework *possible*, I suggest that we should increasingly also look at the conditions which render a particular approach *necessary*. By this I do not mean to promote any rational choice-like ideas that certain solutions are best suited to maximize profits, or meet "interests," of governmental actors. What I mean is that we should be sensitive to hegemonic issues and frames in public discourse and collective memory. These issues are often so important in the public arena that they provide implicit or even explicit answers to the two big questions of collective identities: Where are we coming from?, and Where are we going?. Pertaining to the Israeli case, an example would be what Dan Diner (1998) called the "tribunal character" of Israeli historiography. According to Diner, historiography in Israel has long been dominated by the dichotomy of the accused and the victim. In this storyline, the victim pleads the accused guilty, while the latter tries to diminish her culpability by claiming negligence, not intention. Diner argues that the tribunal has become a dominant way of understanding of how political and historical events and developments are framed in public discourse; it is the glue that connects the past to the present to the future. When discussing the regulation of hESC research, my informants often responded as if Israel was being forced into the role of the accused. "We are proud to be different," one of my informants told me in Tel Aviv in July 2003. The sub-text to this statement is: "we" have nothing to hide or to be ashamed of. Rejecting the role of the accused is a collective necessity, as otherwise the roles in the tribunal frame would be turned upside down, which would render it useless as a source of meaning in the public space. Thus, conditions of necessity signify a situation where the deviation from a particular policy course becomes virtually impossible, because such a deviation would conflict with hegemonic narratives and frames that are so deeply involved in structuring the social and political space that they have become literally vital for the collective. The "tribunal" structure of how historical and political developments are ordered and understood also helps us to understand why the "risk" frame provided by Israeli demographics for how scientific advance is assessed is so effective. In light of, as I argued above, the collective Jewish Israeli body being perceived as in danger, it is the "tribunal" structure of "either/or," namely of being either on the right or on the wrong side; of being either guilty or innocent, that renders risk so actionable. Ignoring the risk to the collective would mean to be on the wrong side of the court room, namely on the side of those standing to be accused for the end of Israel's existence in the Middle East as we know it. Taking the risk to the collective seriously, on the other hand, implies an imperative to do everything possible not only to improve the quality of life of those living in the country, but also to enhance the quantity of those who can contribute to the survival of the Jewish Israeli collective body. The advancement of medical and technological progress serves both of these ends. For Israeli embryos, this means that there are privileged purposes for which they can be used: procreation, or research – both of which aim at the quantitative or qualitative betterment of humans. At the level of collective meaning and memory, this is their *necessary* meaning.

Acknowledgements

I am grateful to Alison Harvey, Frank J. Leavitt, Margaret Sleeboom-Faulkner, and the anonymous referees for very helpful comments on earlier versions of this manuscript. Possible mistakes are mine.

Notes

1. According to the Israeli Central Bureau of Statistics, the 24 IVF clinics in Israel performed close to 28,000 cycles of IVF in 2003 (cf. Simonstein 2008, p. 732; my own informants tell me that because of the absence of a duty to provide documentation of IVF procedures to any central agency, these numbers are unreliable and probably higher).
2. I am grateful to an anonymous referee for pointing out this argument to me.

3. The metaphor of religion seems fitting as trust in science was so strong that it was at times compared with religious faith. For example, this is how the famous pathologist Rudolf Virchow phrased it: "We too have a *creed*, *faith* in the progress of our knowledge of the truth" (cf. Stern 1999, p. 16. See also Efron 2007, p. 167. Emphases added). It is because of this intimate parallel between trust in God and trust in science that Weiss' notion of civil religion seems to capture the dynamics of its workings in Israel better than Jasanoff's brilliant term of "civic epistemologies" which signifies "the institutionalized practices by which members of a given society test knowledge claims used as a basis for making collective choices" (Jasanoff 2005, p. 255).

4. Some very orthodox people are skeptical of the imperative for "higher secular education." This, interestingly, often does not translate into hesitance or hostility towards the fruits of this higher secular education, namely e.g. technological applications. I thank Frank J. Leavitt for alerting me to this point.

References

Barilan, Y.M. and Siegal, G., 2005. The stem cell debate: a Jewish perspective on human dignity, human creativity and inter-religious dialogues. *In*: W. Bender, C. Hauskeller and A. Manzei, eds. *Crossing borders: cultural, political and religious differences concerning stem cell research*. Münster: Agenda Verlag, 231–259.

Baron, S.W., 1952. *A social and religious history of the Jews*. 2nd ed. New York: Columbia University Press.

Birenbaum-Carmeli, D. and Carmeli, Y., eds, 2010. *Kin, gene, community: reproductive technologies among Jewish Israelis*. New York: Berghahn Books.

Cassuto, E., 1961. *A commentary on the Book of Genesis*. Jerusalem: Magnes Press.

Diner, D., 1998. Ereignis und Erinnerung. Über Variationen historischen Gedächtnisses [Event and commemoration. On variations of historical memory]. *In*: B. Faulenbach and B.Schütte B., eds. *Deutschland, Israel und der Holocaust. Zur Gegenwartsbedeutung der Vergangenheit*, [Germany, Israel, and the Holocaust. On the present relevance of history]. Essen: Klartext, 55–70.

Efron, N.J., 2007. *Judaism and science: a historical introduction*. Westport, CT: Greenwood Press.

Eidelman, A.I. and Halperin, M., 2009. The preimplantation embryo and Jewish law. *Nature Medicine*, 15 (3), 238–239.

Eliade, M., 1959. *The sacred and the profane*. New York: Harper and Brothers.

Engelhardt, H.T., 2007. Christian bioethics in a post-Christian age. *Revista Romana de Bioetica*, 5 (1), 5–19.

Feldman, D.M., 1968. *Marital relations, birth control, and abortion in Jewish Law*. New York: New York University Press.

Foa, S., 2002. Battle of the wombs: the future's numbers game. *The Village Voice*, 2 December [online]. Available from: http://www.villagevoice.com/2002-12-03/news/battle-of-the-wombs/ [Accessed December 2010].

Geesink, I., Prainsack, B., and Franklin, S., eds., 2008. Stem cell stories 1998-2008. Special issue. *Science as Culture*, 17 (1).

Gill, R., 2005. Response to: the human embryo in the Christian tradition. *Journal of Medical Ethics*, 31 (12), 713–714.

Goffman, E., 1974. *Frame analysis: an essay on the organization of experience*. New York: Harper & Row.

Green, R.M., 2008. Embryo as epiphenomenon: some cultural, social and economic forces driving the stem cell debate. *Journal of Medical Ethics*, 34 (12), 840–844.

Gross, M.L. and Ravitsky, V., 2003. Israel: bioethics in a Jewish-democratic state. *Cambridge Quarterly of Healthcare Ethics*, 12 (3), 247–255.

Hashiloni-Dolev, Y. and Weiner, N., 2008. New reproductive technologies, genetic counselling and the standing of the fetus: views from Germany and Israel. *Sociology of Health & Illness*, 30 (7), 1055–1069.

IASH (Israeli Academy of Sciences and Humanities), 2001. *The Report of the Bioethics Advisory Committee of the Israeli Academy of Sciences and Humanities on the use of embryonic stem cells for therapeutic research* (August) [online]. Available from: http://bioethics.academy.ac.il/english/report1/Report1-e.html [Accessed December 2010].

Jasanoff, S., 2005. *Designs on nature: science and democracy in Europe and the United States*. Princeton, NJ: Princeton University Press.

Jones, D.A., 2005. The human embryo in the Christian tradition: a reconsideration. *Journal of Medical Ethics*, 31 (12), 710–713.

Kahn, S.M., 2000. *Reproducing Jews: a cultural account of assisted conception in Israel*. Durham, NC: Duke University Press.

Kanaaneh, R.A., 2002. *Birthing the nation: strategies of Palestinian women in Israel*. Berkeley: University of California Press.

Lavi, S., 2008. From bioethics to bio-optics: the case of the embryonic stem cell. *Law, Culture and the Humanities*, 4, 339–351.

Leavitt, F.J., 1998. The concept of nature in Maimonides' philosophy of medicine: Jewish or Greek? *Korot, The Israeli Journal of the History of Medicine and Science*, 13, 102–121.

Margulies, A., 2006. Israel leads world in stem cell research papers per capita, *Israel 21c – Innovation News Service* [online]. Available from: http://www.israel21c.org/index.php?option=com_content&view=article&id=1312&catid=57:health&Itemid=63 [Accessed December 2010]

Metzler, I., 2007. "Nationalizing embryos": the politics of human embryonic stem cell research in Italy. *BioSocieties*, 2, 413–427.

Myskja, B.K., 2009. Rationality and religion in the public debate on embryo stem cell research and prenatal diagnostics. *Medicine, Healthcare and Philosophy*, 12 (2), 213–224.

Penslar, D., 1991. *Zionism and technocracy: the engineering of Jewish settlement in Palestine. 1870–1918*. Bloomington: Indiana University Press.

Prainsack, B., 2006. Negotiating life: the regulation of embryonic stem cell research and human cloning in Israel. *Social Studies of Science*, 36 (2), 173–205.

Prainsack, B. and Firestine, O., 2005. Genetically modified survival: red and green biotechnology in Israel. *Science as Culture*, 14 (4), 355–372.

Prainsack, B. and Firestine, O., 2006. "Science for survival": biotechnology regulation in Israel. *Science and Public Policy*, 33 (1), 33–46.

Prainsack, B., Cherkas, L.F., and Spector, T.D., 2007. Attitudes towards human reproductive cloning, assisted reproduction, and gene selection – a survey of 4,600 British twins. *Human Reproduction*, 22 (8), 2302–2308.

Prainsack, B., Geesink, I., and Franklin, S., eds., 2008. Stem cell technologies 1998–2008: controversies and silences. Special issue. *Science as Culture*, 17 (4).

Schön, D. and Rein, M., 1994. *Frame reflection: toward the resolution of intractable controversies*. New York: Basic Books.

Siegel-Itzkovich, J., 2006. Israeli human embryonic stem cell research is 2nd in world. *The Jerusalem Post*, 6 October [online]. Available from: http://www.jpost.com/HealthAndSci-Tech/Health/Article.aspx?id=36965 [Accessed December 2010].

Simonstein, F., 2008. Embryonic stem cells: the disagreement debate and embryonic stem cell research in Israel. *Journal of Medical Ethics*, 34, 732–734.

Stafford, N., 2006. Stem cell density highest in Israel, *The Scientist*, 21 March [online]. Available from: http://www.the-scientist.com/news/display/23240/ [Accessed December 2010].

Stern, F., 1999. *Einstein's German world*. Princeton, NJ: Princeton University Press.

Weiss, M., 2002. *The chosen body: the politics of the body in Israeli society.* Stanford, CA: Stanford University Press.

Wright, G.E., 1950. *The Old Testament against its environment*. London: SCM Press.

Looking beyond the regulatory exteriors of stem cell research in Asia – discussion

Margaret Sleeboom-Faulkner

Department of Anthropology University of Sussex, Falmer, UK

Literature on the governance of stem cell research often assumes that improved regulation and biopolitical governance will keep stem cell research practices within the bounds of acceptable scientific development. But examples from India, Mainland China, Japan, South Korea, Taiwan and Israel illustrate how formal regulation of stem cell research plays out differently in practice, showing that the standardization of stem cell research in fact creates new spaces in which "unacknowledged" but tolerated stem cell research practices proceed and flourish. The special issue illustrates how in Asian countries, depending on the quality of the research infrastructure, donated embryos and oocytes acquire different values for researchers, and competition in the life sciences requires different attitudes and efforts from scientists. Owing to the varying health needs and investment in the life sciences, disagreement exists about the national values associated with stem cell research, and its importance as a healthcare resource for local populations.

Examples from India, Mainland China, Japan, South Korea, Taiwan and Israel illustrate how the formal regulation of stem cell research plays out variously in its socio-economic and political embedding. Comparing stem cell research conditions in countries that differ in their financial capacity, level of science development, and politico-religious outlook shows that bioethical research regulation acquires variable meanings in informal bioethical practices. Regulatory practices of stem cell research are shaped by a constellation of material and subjective factors, including the availability of research facilities, the ability to attract foreign investment and companies, the wish to maintain a clean reputation, policies for promoting national interests, and the desire to protect human life.

Semi-legal and illegal practices of stem cell research in a clinical setting

In academic literature on the governance of stem cell research (SCR) it is common to proceed from the idea that improved biopolitical governance will keep stem cell research practices within the bounds of acceptable scientific development (Salter 2008, Chen 2009, Glasner 2009, Gottweis 2009). This special issue, however, emphasizes that whether this is so entirely depends on how regulation is channeled through institutional conventions and conditions into the practices of work in the laboratories and hospitals. Thus, the role of the state and the form of institutional management (egalitarian, hierarchical, competitive), the workings of ethics committees and supervision (efficiency, corruptibility), the availability of healthcare resources, and adequate healthcare coverage and patient protection are crucial to the functioning of providers offering stem cell therapies. Thus, the contribution by Priscilla Song in this issue highlights the ways in which private clinics have been ensconced in public hospital premises in Beijing, China, where also public hospitals have entered the socialist market economy since 2000. Song demonstrates how formal regulation in China does not so much encompass the micro-physics of power as tempt scientists to create enterprising strategies that make use of the weak spots in the regulatory system to satisfy other interests, in this case the interests of physicians using lucrative stem cell therapies. Song's research also suggests that rather than producing biopolitical modes of governance, formal regulation in China often invites enterprising tactics and hybrid practices that ultimately remake the boundaries between the public and private, as well as the ethical and unethical, in unexpected ways.

The article by Prasanna Patra and Margaret Sleeboom-Faulkner on the ambiguous symbolism of recruiter-patients as strategic boundary persons in India demonstrates how the institutional set-up of hospitals in these Indian high-tech metropolises of Chennai and Bangalore facilitates the outsourcing of illegal therapies to smaller hospitals hidden in the dense connection networks of large private hospitals. These hospitals often are in private–public partnerships, swallowing up public money, which gets channeled into lucrative illegal practices. As such, a similar institutional set-up obtains to that in Mainland China (see Song in this special issue), where public hospitals, stimulated to make profits, harbor private stem cell therapy providers on their premises. For an increasingly large proportion of healthcare and hospital facilities cater for healthcare for "stem cell tourism." The article shows how "recruiter-patients" are mobilized to draw potential patients into the treatment gambit of clinics. It is the multiple faces of such recruiter-patients that make them "ambiguous symbols": they embody divergent meanings to different publics (including themselves) in the symbol of the cured patient. These clinics strategically use recruiter-patients in asking exorbitant fees for experimental therapies, leading medium incomes families to bankruptcy, in exchange for hope for a better quality of life.

Governing the benefit of embryo and oocyte donation

Human embryonic stem cell research (hESR), even when conducted in accordance with existing regulation for embryo and oocyte donation, raises questions related to the use of scarce financial resources on public health budgets (Dickenson 2007). In Europe, experimental therapies are regarded as expensive (an issue raised by Austin Smith in connection with the high costs associated with stem cell therapy, see *The Guardian*, 30 January 2009), and questions have arisen as to whether it will be possible to scale them up for more general, affordable, use. In large developing countries this issue raises even more painful questions, as central governments channel scarce resources into expensive therapies while basic healthcare is unattainable for the majority of the population (Blumenthal and Hsiao 2005, Zhang and Sleeboom-Faulkner in press). The ethics of the donation of embryos and oocytes for hESR, then, needs to be seen in a different light in high-income and low-income countries. Thus, appealing to the desire of potential donors of oocytes and embryos for research that might in future provide cures for the sick seems cynical in a country where those cures would not reach most of them, because of the limited reach of healthcare provision. Awareness of this fact is becoming increasingly widespread, and obtaining gametes for scientific research for free has become increasingly difficult. Only a few years ago, in India, the dominant discourse defined reproductive resources such as oocytes and embryos as waste (Bharadwaj 2003). But it has become general knowledge that umbilical cords, embryos and oocytes have become valuable to the life sciences as biomaterials.

As shown in the articles by Jyotsna Gupta and Achim Rosemann, embryonic and fetal tissues and oocytes are part of a tissue economy (Waldby and Mitchell 2006) and are disentangled from the socio-economic contexts of couples desperate for a child in IVF clinics. In India, Gupta argues, limited regulation with no legislative authority and ad hoc monitoring has led to a gamut of ethically dubious donation practices, where the ethical arrangements that are supposed to enable donation are largely dependent on the demand for reproductive materials by the life sciences. While still entangled (Callon 1998) in the socio-economic context of the couple, personal and social values are attached to the embryo, oocytes and fetus, although these values are not commonly voiced or heard. Though informed consent for the donation of embryos, oocytes and fetuses is taken, its meaning is not always clear. Achim Rosemann, in his contribution on "the social life of stem cells," shows in a Chinese context that, once disentangled from their "natural" owners, stem cell lines, cells and products start to take on values in the form of research material for articles, exchange material for collaboration, and medical products for medical therapies.

That the future benefits of such research, collaboration and therapies are not likely to reach the majority of the population in need of basic healthcare is of relevance to the value of reproductive biomaterials. Rosemann demonstrates that the current regulation concerning the establishment of human embryonic stem cell lines in China enables the usage of reproductive biomaterials as a source of power, not in the hands of potential patients, but in the laboratories of stem cell researchers. Stem cell researchers, Rosemann argues, use them strategically to accrue various forms of influence and values. Control over biomaterials makes stem cell researchers attractive as collaborative partners vis-à-vis other researchers, strengthens their bargaining position, and, when applied successfully, adds to their prestige. As such, a fundamental rift exists between values attached to embryos among embryo donors in the context of IVF, and the values generated by the use of donated embryonic tissues. More attention, then, should be paid to the place such donations occupy in the overall ambitions of scientists and governments to be among the vanguard of international cutting-edge stem cell research.

National ambition, international competition and stem cell research in a local setting

Stem cell research has lent itself as a means for attaining national glory and to acquire a place among the world's advanced nations in the life sciences (cf. Gottweis 2009). These ambitions, however, entail enormous costs in developing countries with a limited budget and in small countries, which can hardly afford the elaborate regulatory and scientific infrastructure needed for the enablement of cutting-edge innovative stem cell research at a global level. In both cases emphasis on the development of a small area of science is obtained by proportionally high investment, sending the country's most promising talents abroad for training, and tempting them back with the promise of good jobs in advanced labs with state-of-the-art facilities also imported from abroad. In such situations, the question arises how existing institutions translate these semi-imported science projects and regulatory devices into potentially successful stem cell practices domestically.

Pertaining to this question, Joy Zhang in her article on scientific institutions and governance in China asks how Chinese academic infrastructures interact with the institutional requirements of stem cell research. Zhang discovered that in many Chinese laboratories the middle layer of researchers – that between professor and research student – is missing, and that the structure of scientific institutions lacks professional diversity and teambuilding. Furthermore, the fierce competition between research institutions, the competition for the top job of principal investigator (PI) and the shortage of low-paid jobs in the middle layer mean that the Chinese world of SCR has a disadvantage in the competition to become a global player in SCR. Zhang illustrates also how the current lack of coordination between the Ministries of Health and of Science and Technology has led to insufficient coherence of science policies to ensure effective consistency of stem cell governance in practice. This case study suggests that without the infrastructural means and an institutional culture conducive to it, even when funding and highly educated researchers are available, international ambition for regenerative medicine may be difficult to realize.

Raising similar questions about stem cell research governance, the article by Leo Kim on the knowledge economy of stem cell research in South Korea shows how dog-eat-dog competition in the South Korean life sciences undermines the autonomy of science and democratic reflection upon scientific practice. Kim argues that to attain a world leading position in stem cell research, not only were data fabricated and female researchers subjected to ovary hyper-stimulation and egg donation, the entire working regime and atmosphere in the stem cell laboratory were cross-fertilized by parochial political cultures of paternalistic attitudes. Despite avowed commitments to more rational and democratic research practice at the institutional level, competition and harsh working regimes are internalized in the local governance of life sciences in South Korea. Kim raises the question of whether such "neo-liberal" competition, expressed in the high work pressure in laboratories, in the end will yield a form of science that people can be proud of.

The paradoxes of ageing welfare societies: donation, high-tech and regulation

While the distribution of resources for research and healthcare is a main concern in developing countries, it is a concern, too, in affluent welfare societies, and it has taken on new priority since the "ageing society" became an item high on the public health agenda. One of the reasons for stimulating hESR in Japan has been to find cures for degenerative diseases for the elderly in an ageing society (Cyranoski 2002). But the need for human reproductive materials has created a burden for women and has led to discussions on the ethics of donating embryos and ova. Even though the issue of ova and embryo donation has not attracted the dramatic media attention that it has in the USA, South Korea or Europe, the debate seems to have been taken seriously by policymakers. Margaret Sleeboom-Faulkner shows that although the regulatory regime of hESR in Japan is similarly permissive of creating stem cell lines, the details of the regulation for the use of embryonic stem cell lines and therapeutic cloning have been followed to the letter of the guidelines. The sensitivity of the bureaucracy to scandal and critical civic players in Japanese society have led researchers to seek other ways of producing pluripotency. In 2006, this effort succeeded in the form of induced pluripotent stem (iPS) cells. Ironically, the nationalist sentiments that accompanied the discovery of iPS cells have led to concrete measures of lowering the bureaucratic wall of procedures for gaining permission to work with human embryonic stem cells. This has also led to a reshuffling of notions of ethics, scandal, safety and risk linked to both kinds of research. For becoming the first to successfully apply human embryonic stem cell therapy in a clinical setting has become a national target and an aim of the newly set up intellectual property rights regime for stem cell research. But in segments of Japanese society ideas associated with modern science, such as fierce competition, rationalization and the lengthening of life are associated with Western instrumentalism. Thus, a number of handicapped and women's groups, politicians and scientists are asking questions about the costs society is prepared to pay to save and "artificially" lengthen the lives of individuals in terms of what is regarded as "unnatural" in Japanese culture.

In South Korea the issue of oocyte donation has attracted much attention, both nationally and internationally. The media depict women in South Korea as eager to donate ova. The article by Azumi Tsuge and Hyunsoo Hong on the paradox surrounding women as "voluntary egg donors" in South Korea explains why South Korean women should be seen neither as victims of unreasonable demands or deceit, nor as free decision-makers, as they frequently have been portrayed in the press. On the basis of interviews with women and patient organizations, participation in seminars on stem cell research, and by focusing on the women's lives rather than on the act of donation, Tsuge and Hong shed new light on the motivation of women to donate ova. They describe the egg donors in their gender relation within South Korean society, and as part of the dynamic world of competitive scientific enterprise promoted through global and local politics. Where technological means play an increasingly important role in people's reproductive lives and in their old age, it becomes clear that the driving forces of these women to donate ova reach further than mere nationalism or blackmail.

Representations of society, communities of fate, and biological citizenship

Considering the many socio-economic and political questions playing a role in the regulation of stem cell research, an important question is how society decides what is bioethical. One problem is that citizens are more interested in some topics than in others, and governments' and scientists' views on the role of the public in the regulation of science research vary. Furthermore, there are many ways of representing the public, and limited possibilities of taking into account the views of all citizens. While some science topics are simply too complex for a general audience of laypeople to understand, in some countries citizens may have well-informed views about a subject, but do not believe that the government takes their views seriously.

It is clear, therefore, that there are various ways in which people define their views on stem cell research vis-à-vis their governments. On the basis of research among people from various religious denominations and scientific experts in different fields of stem cell research, Jennifer Liu in her article on "biological scarcity" and research progress in Taiwan demonstrates how new notions of peoplehood are increasingly based on biological imaginations of self, family, and nation, that is, biological citizenship. These notions do not necessarily correspond to a "Westernization" or "individualization" of the Taiwanese people. For responses to stem cell science vary widely: private cord stem cell banking flourishes thanks to an emphasis on furthering the interests of the family; bone marrow banking is successful especially as a result of the formation of a shared "community of fate" (Ong and

Chen 2010, pp. 19–21; 33–38); and the Taiwan biobank has been unsuccessful, due especially to a distrust of government. So how, in the midst of such complexity, can we conclude what is bioethical to whom? The Taiwan case shows that different identities (family, community, state) and different ethical issues seem to be important depending on what kinds of stem cell research are at stake; cord cell banking, bone marrow banking or embryonic stem cell banking pertain to different bioethical issues involving different aspects of society.

Critics have often censured the forcing of Western moral values, such as respect for the human embryo, upon non-Western countries. The pressure to regulate hESR in Asia, then, would be aimed at augmenting respect for the human embryo as a precious form of life. However, such presumptions ignore the question of why regulation of hESR is important, and to whom. This question of social representation Barbara Prainsack tackles in her article on the public basis for the regulation of embryonic stem cell research in Israel. Prainsack critically observes a tendency among academic authors to project their own ideologies and ideals in their analysis of the bioethical situation in other countries, while failing to detect, recognize or accept alternative explanations for the development, creation and adherence to certain bioethical beliefs. The case of Zionist endorsement of scientific and technological progress, according to Prainsack, undermines the "deficit model" of public understanding of science and demonstrates that, as is the case in Liu's case study on Taiwan, science research acquires meaning in the lives of the public in particular socio-political contexts, in which "culture" and "religion" may or may not play a role (among many other factors). Therefore, the realization of the complexity of representing social, economic, religious and political interest groups in interaction with historical factors and global trends should provide the authors of papers on public attitudes towards stem cell research with a due dose of caution, self-reflection and restraint, for any document in this field is no more than a fragment of a necessary, but at the same time, ongoing and incomplete discussion.

Discussion

Case studies in the special double issue on the various aspects of stem cell research in Asian countries show that formal regulation of stem cell research practices, including oocyte and embryo donation, stem cell research in the laboratory, and clinical applications of stem cell therapies, play out differently according to the society in which they are adopted. Formal research regulation therefore cannot be equated with its implementation. Understanding the way regulation actually works requires intimate knowledge of the existing modes of social control, media and functioning of local, provincial and national authorities. Research regulation is often not implemented as intended, as shown in the case of oocyte donation in India, South Korea and China (Gupta, Kim, Song). In fact, the existence of formal regulation may invite a range of hybrid practices, trigger unintended consequences or have little effect. Thus, Song showed that formal regulation invites new strategies of scientists making use of the weaknesses in the regulation, allowing dubious private practices to flourish under recognized public healthcare institutions; Patra and Sleeboom-Faulkner showed how public–private partnerships, using public money and the more reliable image of "public research," may harbor underground stem cell therapies buried in large contact networks. In this maze of connections, dubious practices of using "recruiter-patients" can thrive disregards and sometimes thanks to the existence of formal regulation disallowing them; Gupta and Kim showed that rogue ethical practices around oocyte and embryo donation depend not so much on the bioethical awareness of regulation, but rather on their demand. Thus, when the demand for oocytes and embryos is high in an environment ruled by fierce competition in the life sciences, and if violation of the regulation is not checked, then ethics education and ethical awareness have little impact on donation practices; the case of applying relatively permissive regulation of hESR in Japan showed that the extreme caution of civil servants in practice leads to a decline in scientific activity in the area, which was not intended by the regulators. And, finally, Tsuge and Hong showed that bioethical regulation for oocyte donation based on individual informed consent is not workable when confronted with volunteers motivated by a social and public spirit of sacrifice and belief in scientific progress.

The question of the variable and unintended effects of regulation around stem cell research is closely related to the questions of who benefits from the research, how its implementation benefits those working on stem cell research, and how the benefits of stem cell research are channeled to patient populations. Zhang, Tsuge and Hong, and Kim related how national benefit is an important basis for investing in stem cell research. This goal differs from the aim of providing the population with the benefits of the research. Thus, research based on donated embryos and oocytes in India and Mainland China is not likely to benefit the majority of patients, as healthcare provisions are very basic and mainly benefit privileged groups. Rather, embryo and oocyte donation especially benefits the careers of stem cell researchers, private hospitals and public–private enterprises. In the case of South Korea, Tsuge and Hong demonstrated how oocyte and embryo donation is motivated by women who define themselves in terms of gender relations and, in the name of country and the sick, feel they are obliged to help science. Liu showed in her case study on biocitizenship in Taiwan, how who benefits from the research largely depends on the kinds of stem cell technology in question, as they can benefit the family, the individual, certain ethnic groups or the nation as a whole. In the case of Japan, Sleeboom-Faulkner indicated that although investment in hESR was motivated to repair the consequences of an ageing society, questions have been raised about the ethical boundary between helping those in urgent need of new cures and keeping the aged alive artificially against their wishes. Prainsack's article draws our attention to how attitudes towards hESR are not necessarily motivated by bioethics, cultural or religious dogma, but may actually be based on a belief in science. The reasons for supporting science research were also referred to in the articles by Kim, Liu, Tsuge and Hong and Sleeboom-Faulkner, and raise questions about the representation of public needs, research motivation, resource allocation, bioethics regulation and safety. For, after all, the investment in stem cell research needs to be justified by fair and transparent representations of what populations need, what researchers research, and what bioethics protects.

So to what extent can we say whether the establishment of imported regulatory concepts and concepts of governance is successful? In the areas of private stem cell research, the case studies by Song, Gupta, and Patra and Sleeboom-Faulkner confirmed that the motives for stem cell research are often profit, rather than scientific understanding. Although regulation has made lucrative human experimentation practices illegal, this does not visibly limit them in practice. Song's case study even demonstrates that regulation in China's science establishment invited new, hybrid forms of research that remain out of the reach of government control. In fact, it could be argued that implementation of regulation is not always a political priority. Scientific progress in stem cell research, however, has become an important national target in the light of global competition in the life sciences. But Kim, in his review of the science community in South Korea, asks the very basic question of whether in a science community of dog-eat-dog competition stem cell research is something to be proud of, even if it is successful. This question leads to another issue in need of further research: How investment into stem cell research variously and unequally benefits the interests of public health, the stem cell research community, and scientific understanding.

References

Bharadwaj, A., 2003. Why adoption is not an option in India: the visibility of infertility, the secrecy of donor insemination, and other cultural complexities. *Social Science & Medicine*, 56, 1867–1880.

Blumenthal, D. and Hsiao, W., 2005. Privatization and its discontents: the evolving Chinese health care system. *New England Journal of Medicine*, 353 (11), 1165–1170.

Callon, M., 1999. Actor-network theory – the market test. *In*: J. Law and J. Hassard, eds. *Actor network theory and after*. Oxford: Blackwell.

Chen, H., 2009. Stem cell governance in China: from bench to bedside? *New Genetics and Society*, 28 (3), 267–282.

Cyranoski, D., 2002. Japanese science: rebirth and regeneration. *Nature*, 415, 952–953.

Dickenson, D., 2007. *Property in the body: feminist perspectives*. Cambridge: Cambridge University Press.

Glasner, P., 2009. Cellular division: social and political complexity in Indian stem cell research. *New Genetics and Society*, 28 (3), 283–296.

Gottweis, H., 2009. Editorial: biopolitics in Asia. *New Genetics and Society*, 28 (3), 201–204.

The Guradian, 2009. Medical marvels, The Guardian, 30 January 2009 [online]. Available at: http://www.guardian.co.uk/science/2009/jan30/stemcells-genetics [Accessed 30 June 2011].

Ong, A. and Chen, N., eds., 2010. *Asian biotechnology: population, security, & nation*. Duke University Press.

Salter, B., 2008. Governing stem cell science in China and India: emerging economies and the global politics of innovation. *New Genetics and Society*, 27 (2), 145–159.

Waldby, C. and Mitchell, R., 2006. *Tissue economies: blood, organs, and cell lines in late capitalism.* Durham, NC: Duke University Press.

Zhang, X. and Sleeboom-Faulkner, M., in press. Tensions between medical professionals and patients in Mainland China: issues of communication, trust and medical provisions. *Cambridge Quarterly of Healthcare Ethics.*

Index

Note: Page numbers in **bold** type refer to figures
Page numbers followed by 'n' refer to notes